I0085057

Interior Format
© **KILLION**
THE GROUP INC.

Mondays *with* Jesus

2017

Devotions to Start Each Week with Your Savior

RENEE ANDREWS

MONDAY, JANUARY 2

66 *I SAW THE HOLY CITY, THE new Jerusalem, coming down out of heaven from God, prepared as a bride beautifully dressed for her husband. And I heard a loud voice from the throne saying, "Look! God's dwelling place is now among the people, and he will dwell with them. They will be his people, and God himself will be with them and be their God. 'He will wipe every tear from their eyes. There will be no more death' or mourning or crying or pain, for the old order of things has passed away." Revelation 21:2-4*

A dear friend is traveling this week and sent a photo she took from the window seat of the plane. She titled it, "The view above the clouds." I was amazed at the beauty, at the way the white clouds looked golden beneath the sun, the way the sky positioned between the sun and clouds mirrored Caribbean blue water and at the way my heart felt peace, simply by admiring the perfection of God's beauty.

I don't fly as often as I used to, but I always thought that picturesque view probably resembled the scene in Heaven. I imagined those streets of gold, transparent as glass, pearly white gates, city walls covered in precious jewels. That was surely the best way to describe the beauty of Heaven.

But then I realized…I was so very wrong. The true beauty of Heaven won't have anything to do with pearly gates, golden streets or jeweled walls, and for me to equate it to such things—things—devalues the magnitude of beauty God has planned for us at His Home. Because the true beauty of Heaven isn't described in the verses that center Revelation 21. It's described in those verses above:

There will be no more tears, no more death, no more mourning, no more pain. And the ultimate true beauty of Heaven is that God will dwell among His people. He will *dwell* among *us*! Praise God! I can't imagine anything more beautiful than that!

This Week: Get up early enough to see the sun rise, at least once. Plan your evening to see the sun set, at least once. Imagine that the night never comes, and neither do tears, of suffering or pain. Thank God that, in your future, you will encounter a day where the sun never sets!

MY PRAYER TO START THIS WEEK:

_____

_____

_____

_____

_____

_____

THOSE TO REMEMBER IN PRAYER THIS WEEK:

_____

_____

_____

_____

_____

_____

_____

MONDAY, JANUARY 9

" *GOING A LITTLE FARTHER, HE fell with his face to the ground and prayed, "My Father, if it is possible, may this cup be taken from me. Yet not as I will, but as you will." Matthew 26:39*

My husband likes old cars, particularly old Mustangs. He has a '67 Mustang (that's about all I know about it, but he could give you a ton of car lingo that would mean something to car enthusiasts). Recently, he bought a '92 Mustang convertible that had seen better days. It didn't run. In fact, we could hardly find anything on the car that worked. However, it was priced at $300, so my sweet Cajun decided it was worth the investment. He tinkered with it for months, rebuilding an engine to get it running again and replacing almost every part that formed the car.

Eventually, I needed to run errands, and that Mustang was my car of choice. I was impressed at how well it ran, given we'd had it towed to the house. But I quickly learned that the vehicle was still a work in progress.

After completing my errands, I started home. That's when the skies turned dark, and rain poured down. Not an ordinary rain, but the kind that comes with a severe thunderstorm of tornadic proportions. Unfortunately, this was when I realized my husband had yet to put the wipers back on the car. The air, heat and defroster also hadn't been fixed yet, and the windows started fogging with the changing temperature. Luckily, I was able to roll the windows down, but that only caused the rain to dump all over me as I squinted through the storm and attempted to find a shoulder on the side of the road where I could park the car until the storm passed.

The biggest problem? I had just started across a bridge with no shoulder when the rain began. I couldn't see the lines on the road. I couldn't tell when the bridge ended. My hazard lights didn't work. I slowed the car to a near crawl as I tried to see, which only caused other cars to zoom past and send more water through the window.

Years ago, I would have yelled. Or cried. And I did cry, but my cries were to my Father. "Lord, don't let it happen this way. This isn't how I want to die." An eighteen wheeler passed me, and I honestly could no longer see. The windshield was completely fogged over. And I continued praying. I put one arm out of the window and began waving it up and down, as if this might let the other cars know my dilemma. And maybe it did, because they all slowed and stayed behind me, allowing me to marginally see the path ahead well enough to tell when the bridge ended, and when I could safely ease over to the shoulder.

But even then, as I came to a standstill, I prayed. I thanked God for being there through the storm, and I thanked Him for answering my prayer. I did think there was a chance I'd be hit, that my car would be pushed over the side of that bridge or that an eighteen wheeler would crash into me at any moment. But my Lord granted my request. I didn't want to die that way, and I didn't.

And then I thought about Christ's request, when He prayed to His Father at Gethsemane. He asked for the cup to be taken from Him. He asked God not to die that way. But unlike me, when I prayed through my journey across that bridge, Christ didn't merely ask not to die that way. He also prayed that God's will be done. And unlike me, He wasn't facing a mere death that would lead me into a blissful eternity. The cup He asked God to take away was my sin. And all sin. The sin of the world. Placed upon Christ, the Perfect One, the only man who had never sinned.

The pain of what He bore that day is unimaginable. And He knew it would be. Unlike me, in my pitiful trek with the Mustang, Christ knew what would surely happen. He knew what would come and the agony He would face at the cross. But He still prayed…Thy will, not Mine.

And He still went to the cross.

This Week: Reflect on the cross, on the pain that came with the weight of our sin, and on the prayer where Christ asked for that cup to pass...but also asked that His Father's will be done. End each of your prayers this week with, "Thy will be done."

MY PRAYER TO START THIS WEEK:

_____

_____

_____

_____

_____

THOSE TO REMEMBER IN PRAYER THIS WEEK:

_____

_____

_____

_____

_____

_____

_____

MONDAY, JANUARY 16

" "*I PRAYED FOR THIS CHILD, AND the Lord has granted me what I asked of him.*" *1 Samuel 1:27*

As I sit rocking my youngest grandson, I read this notable verse, beautifully displayed on a large wooden sign above his crib. I've seen the verse often, when new parents send a birth announcement or post the baby's photograph on social media. And each time I rock Konrad and read the verse, I know that it is true. We truly prayed for this precious little angel, and God granted our request.

But then I think about a dear friend, who has also prayed for a child, yet she has suffered through three miscarriages, the last one far enough along that she knew she'd have had a baby girl. And then a family member who also desperately wanted to have a child and had four pregnancies, all to end when she stopped feeling her babies move and learned that she had lost another child before ever truly meeting him or her.

They prayed too, and undoubtedly, God also heard their requests. But for some reason, the answers to their prayers were either, "No," or "Not yet."

In one of those cases, the husband and wife turned to each other and to God to find their way through the difficult struggle of losing a child. In the other, they turned away from each other, their marriage in tatters from the strain, and they turned away from God.

I do not know why God answers some prayers with yes and others with no or not yet. But I know that He does answer, and I know that He cares. I also know that I can pray for those who do not get the answers they desire, for their understanding and for them to turn to God for the peace they need in the storm.

Have I prayed for God to miraculously heal someone and yet held that loved one's hand as they passed on to their reward? Absolutely. Have I prayed for a particular job? Yes. Have I prayed for scholarships for my children (years ago, but still…). Yes. Have I prayed for the future spouses of my children, and now of my grandchildren? Definitely.

Did God answer all of my prayers with a yes? No, He didn't.

But I do not doubt that He heard them all, and I do not doubt that He loves me and knows what is best for me, even when I cannot understand. I also know that the prayers of those who prayed for children and didn't receive the children they wanted…were not unheard by our Lord. And I know that He cares for them, and I believe that they will meet those little boys and girls one day in Heaven.

This Week: Undoubtedly, you know someone who has lost a child, either before the baby was born or after. Buy a card of cheer for them. Remind them that you care…and that God cares too. Let them know that you're praying for them, and then pray for them each day. Pray for God to wrap His arms around them, to give them peace and, if it be His will, to fill that void in their lives with a child. Adoption is always a beautiful option and the manner in which I gained two of my precious grandchildren. It's a beautiful thing, isn't it? God adopted us, and it doesn't get more beautiful than that!

MY PRAYER TO START THIS WEEK:

_____

_____

_____

_____

_____

THOSE TO REMEMBER IN PRAYER THIS WEEK:

_____

_____

_____

_____

_____

_____

_____

MONDAY, JANUARY 23

"THEREFORE HE IS ABLE TO *save completely those who come to God through him, because he always lives to intercede for them.*" *Hebrews 7:25*

Last week, Ariel, my daughter-in-law, had several items to put in her car as she was preparing to leave her house for the day. While Naomi, our nine-month-old granddaughter played just inside the door, Ariel took her purse, the diaper bag and some other items o the car. Then she returned to the house to get her little girl…and realized she'd accidentally locked the door.

She ran to the side door, which has a window, and peered in to see Naomi, crawling around, happy as she could be. Ariel tapped on the window, got her little girl's attention, and Naomi smiled, clueless mommy couldn't come in.

With no spare key and her phone still inside the house, Ariel began to panic. She thought about going to a neighbor's home to use the phone, but she was fairly certain that her neighbors were all at work. Then she thought about attempting to break through the window to get to her little girl. But she wasn't certain how that would fare either. What if Naomi crawled toward the glass, or if Ariel cut herself badly in the process?

Deciding her best option was to find a neighbor at home, she prayed for help, ran to her car, sat in the driver's seat and glanced down to see the key that our son, Rene, had left in the cup holder. She began thanking God immediately as she grabbed the key and ran to the door to get to her baby girl.

When Ariel told me the story, I could feel her anxiety. She knew she had to get to Naomi, but she didn't know how…until she found that key.

Aren't we like Ariel, when we know what we want, what we need to get to more than anything else, and yet we need the key?

What do we want to get to most?

God.

What is the key to getting to God?

Christ.

He is our interceder, our path to the Father. He is our means to getting what we need most, what we want most, what will give us more joy than we can ever imagine.

To get to her daughter, Ariel needed the key.

To get to our Heavenly Father, we need Christ.

Thankfully, He is there, waiting to intercede, wanting us to gain access to what we need most. To give us even more joy than Ariel found when she opened that door and found her baby, safe on the other side.

This Week: Make a spare key for your home. Put it somewhere safe, but a place that you would remember if you're ever locked out. Whenever you look at the key, remember the Key we have to access the door to our Father. Thank God for Christ's ability to intercede.

MY PRAYER TO START THIS WEEK:

THOSE TO REMEMBER IN PRAYER THIS WEEK:

MONDAY, JANUARY 30

"*OPEN MY EYES THAT I may see wonderful things in your law.*"
Psalm 119:18

In the early and mid 1990s, I, as well as a large portion of the world, became rather obsessed with stereograms, those images that allow some people to see 3D images by focusing on 2D patterns. This form of art is identified by a horizontally repeating pattern which differs slightly with each repetition, therefore giving the illusion of depth when each eye focuses on a different part of the pattern.

The Magic Eye books that were filled with these stereograms hit the bestseller lists in record time, and entire stores were devoted to selling the popular 3D art. I remember spending the majority of a Saturday morning in such a store in New Orleans attempting to see images like the Statue of Liberty and rockets hidden in a bounty of posters.

When I read Psalm 119:18, I am reminded of those stereograms. There is so much splendor in the Word of God, but often, we are unable to see the beauty that is only obtained by looking deeply into the scripture. More than that, I'm reminded that I can't see the wonders of God's word without His help. I need Him to open my eyes, to allow me to see more, to understand more, to appreciate the awesome jewel that He has given me by providing me with His Word.

This Week: Find a stereogram and search for the hidden image beneath. Feel that moment of triumph, excitement and satisfaction when the veiled figure comes into view. Next, pray for God to open your eyes to the hidden beauty of the scripture, then spend time in His Word. Take a look at 2 Corinthians 3. Read about how you are a letter from Christ, written not with ink but with the Spirit of the living God, not on tablets of stone, but on tablets of human heart. Start there, and then delve into more scripture, into more hidden beauty. Have your eyes opened to the wonders of God's Word.

MY PRAYER TO START THIS WEEK:

_____

_____

_____

_____

_____

THOSE TO REMEMBER IN PRAYER THIS WEEK:

_____

_____

_____

_____

_____

_____

_____

MONDAY, FEBRUARY 6

" *FATHERS, DO NOT EMBITTER YOUR children, or they will become discouraged. Whatever you do, work at it with all your heart, as working for the Lord, not for human masters, since you know that you will receive an inheritance from the Lord as a reward. It is the Lord Christ you are serving.*"
Colossians 3:21, 23-24

Growing up, I remember a worn brown grocery sack as a steady constant on our dryer. Though Mom often exchanged the bag with a fresh one from the grocery store, the smell of its contents lingered in the small laundry room next to our carport.

The scent of rubber or, more accurately, of a tire plant.

My Daddy, James Bowers, worked at Goodyear for thirty-seven years. He began building tires at merely twenty years old, working third shift for years before finally moving to days. The work was labor intensive, to say the least. Back then, we had one car, and Momma would drive us to the plant to watch the men pouring out when their shift ended. My sister and I would search for the familiar walk of the man who provided everything we needed, the man who loved us unconditionally…and never complained about the position that would send him home with the potent scent of the tire plant on his clothes.

Even though it has been decades since that brown bag stayed on the dryer, I remember the scent vividly and would recognize it instantly even now, years later. It's a reminder of what my Daddy was willing to do for us, every day, without complaining. It's a reminder of his love for his wife and children.

As I read the verses above, I realize that Daddy never made us feel bitter toward the plant, but instead made sure we knew how thankful he was for the opportunity to work. And Daddy didn't go to work and leave his Lord at home. The men and women who worked with him through those years knew that he wasn't there alone; he worked with God in his mind and in his heart and didn't hold back from sharing his Lord with his coworkers at the plant.

This Week: If your current employment isn't what you had planned for your-self, or it isn't as appealing as you would like, look at what it provides, rather than what it prevents. Look at it the way my precious Daddy did, as an opportunity, rather than a hindrance. And remember that you aren't in that position to serve man, but to serve your Lord.

MY PRAYER TO START THIS WEEK:

_____

_____

_____

_____

_____

THOSE TO REMEMBER IN PRAYER THIS WEEK:

_____

_____

_____

_____

_____

_____

_____

MONDAY, FEBRUARY 13

" CONSEQUENTLY, YOU ARE NO LONGER *foreigners and strangers, but fellow citizens with God's people and also members of his household.*" Ephesians 2:19

Each year, our extended family gets together for the traditional family reunion. When my Granny Bowers was living, she would organize the event, which always took place at Noccalula Falls, a beautiful park near my hometown that features a 90-foot waterfall, trails and playgrounds for children. It's a stunning place to visit, but even more so when you consider that your family members will travel from all over to gather together and enjoy a meal, visit and catch up on life each year.

I always enjoy seeing the new babies (grandbabies in my case), meeting those who have recently joined the family through marriage, etc. Occasionally, I'll have to pull my mom or dad aside and ask someone's name (everyone changes a little with age, and my memory sure isn't what it used to be.) But this year, two men joined the event that *no one* recognized. And I wasn't the only person pulling others aside to find out the identity of the newcomers.

Eventually, we realized that my cousin Lisa, who now organizes the reunion, had inadvertently tagged the two on Facebook, because they happened to have the same last name as our family. And so they saw the invitation, brought a covered dish, and drove an hour to attend a reunion with a family they had never met. (You can laugh – we all did.) But what was even more interesting is that, after talking with the two for a while, we learned that we really are related...way on down the line.

One day, we will gather, like these men, with a family that we haven't met before, but a family that shares our name. Christians. And what an amazing family reunion that will be!

This Week: Call a family member that you haven't seen in a while. Feel the excitement of reconnecting, learning about everything that has happened in their life, and then imagine reconnecting with your family members that have passed on…and with all of the amazing family you haven't even met! Praise God!

MY PRAYER TO START THIS WEEK:

THOSE TO REMEMBER IN PRAYER THIS WEEK:

MONDAY, FEBRUARY 20

"PREACH THE WORD; BE PREPARED *in season and out of season; correct, rebuke and encourage—with great patience and careful instruction. For the time will come when people will not put up with sound doctrine. Instead, to suit their own desires, they will gather around them a great number of teachers to say what their itching ears want to hear. They will turn their ears away from the truth and turn aside to myths." 2 Timothy 4:2-4*

As a writer, I am continually researching topics and attending meetings and workshops to learn more about subject matter related to my books. Since I also write suspense novels, I have spent quite a bit of time taking courses in forensics and interviewing law enforcement officers, so that my characters and my stories are as accurate as possible.

More than sitting in a classroom and taking notes, I enjoy speaking personally to the detectives involved with cases that are similar to my storylines. I also enjoy listening to the banter they have between each other, seeing the real people behind the badge, so that I can make certain my characters are as "real" as possible.

In speaking to two detectives about their job, I learned that one of them had his photo in the local newspaper more than any other detective at the station, a fact he was rather proud of. But then his partner laughed and explained that he was only in the paper so often because of his ability to point.

Then he explained, "Whenever he sees a photographer from the local paper arrive, he will point toward something at the scene. Nothing substantial, just pointing to anything. It can be a rock, a leaf, or a piece of dirt. But every time, without fail, the reporter will snap the picture and then print it, saying something about detectives finding evidence at the scene."

I then learned that the well-photographed detective had actually lined his office walls with such photos.

While this made me laugh, it also made me think about those who will point to something as if it is fact and how others will believe the fiction because they never searched to find the truth. It's tempting to follow this reasoning in our quest to know more about God's Word, to see someone who appears to know what they are talking about and believe that they're pointing to something worthy, when in fact, we're only directed toward a lie. Something as insubstantial as that rock, leaf or piece of dirt. And something that will not bring us any closer whatsoever to our Savior.

This Week: Have you heard a great sermon lately? If yes, then…Awesome! I love a great sermon! And now that you've heard one, take your notes, pull out your Bible and verify the facts. Delve deeper into what you've heard and increase your knowledge of the scripture. Don't rely on someone else pointing a finger to what they deem as important. Enjoy spending your own time in God's Word.

MY PRAYER TO START THIS WEEK:

_____

_____

_____

_____

_____

THOSE TO REMEMBER IN PRAYER THIS WEEK:

_____

_____

_____

_____

_____

_____

MONDAY, FEBRUARY 27

" IN SPITE OF ALL THIS, *they kept on sinning; in spite of his wonders, they did not believe. So he ended their days in futility and their years in terror. Whenever God slew them, they would seek him; they eagerly turned to him again. They remembered that God was their Rock, that God Most High was their Redeemer.*" *Psalm 78:32-35*

For our twenty-fifth anniversary, J.R. and I traveled across the country on a motorcycle. We brought a small tent and stayed at state parks and campgrounds along the way, truly enjoying the beautiful world God created. On almost every evening, we would find a place to camp without problem; however, we hadn't considered that Memorial Day happened to fall within the span of our travel.

On Memorial Day, like every other day, we rode the bike until dark and then began looking for a place to stay. Unfortunately, there was nowhere to be found. Exhausted and feeling a little defeated, we drove through a tiny town in Arkansas, and the police had a routine traffic stop taking place, where they were checking for licenses and registrations. Blessedly, the officer who checked our forms asked where we were staying and, learning we didn't have a place to go, told us about a tiny campground nearby.

We gratefully went to the campground, set up the tent and quickly went to sleep. And about an hour later, we learned why this campground still had spots available. J.R. and I were in a deep sleep when the earth began to shake, a loud wail pierced the night and a light that nearly blinded us lit up the tent. The officer had forgotten to mention that a train track ran through the center of the campground; he also forgot to mention that a train came through every other hour through the night.

Needless to say, we didn't get much sleep that night, and we still laugh about those abrupt moments when it seemed as though the world was ending…and then the train passed.

Often, in our daily walks of life, we tend to get settled in our ways. We are still breathing, but for the most part, sleeping. We aren't paying attention the way we should, to our God or to His children. And I wonder if God doesn't sometimes have to send a train to wake us up and make us pay attention.

Have you ever thought about all of those miracles God performed in Egypt when He freed the Israelites, and how quickly they forgot His power? Psalm 78 details what God had done for His people: dividing the sea and leading them through, standing water up like a wall, guiding them with a cloud by day and fire at night, splitting rocks in the wilderness to provide water. Yet they forgot. And God woke them up, sending the ark of His might into captivity, His splendor into the hands of the enemy and giving His people over to the sword (verses 61-62).

When something happens in your life that causes you to surrender, to bow your head and turn your life back to the One who gave it, maybe the situation that you're encountering can prove to be the train that you need to wake you up.

This Week: If you're like me, you'll probably have at least one day where you feel completely exhausted, like you can't wait to fall into bed and like you could probably sleep for twenty-four hours straight. This doesn't merely happen from physical exhaustion, but also mental and emotional strain. Now think about that moment when you wake again, after you've had the necessary sleep and are refreshed and prepared for what the new day offers. Thank God for waking you up. And if, like me, something has recently brought you to your knees, caused you to turn back to the One who made you…thank God again, for waking you up.

MY PRAYER TO START THIS WEEK:

_____

_____

_____

_____

_____

THOSE TO REMEMBER IN PRAYER THIS WEEK:

_____

_____

_____

_____

_____

_____

_____

MONDAY, MARCH 6

" FOLLOW GOD'S EXAMPLE, THEREFORE, AS *dearly loved children and walk in the way of love, just as Christ loved us and gave himself up for us as a fragrant offering and sacrifice to God." Ephesians 5:1-2*

I had to wait for the tears to stop before I could write this devotion. Sometimes, you read or hear a story that touches your heart so completely that you are moved to tears. That has happened to me this morning.

As an organ donor, I'm genuinely drawn to stories of organ donation, but even more when the story involves a child's life. Today, I read the story of a family in Alabama whose baby boy had heart failure shortly after birth. He was the youngest patient in the United States to use a Berlin heart, a device that helps pump blood while the infant awaits a heart transplant. His mother said they never prayed for a heart, because they knew praying for a heart was praying for something tragic to happen to another baby.

Four months later, in Louisiana, another family did have something tragic happen, when their six-month-old little boy began running a mysterious fever, and doctors found him to have bleeding on the brain. His parents prayed for a miracle, but during the surgery to stop the bleeding, doctors determined major malformations that couldn't be repaired. Before the doctors took their son off life support, the couple was asked if they wanted to donate his organs.

Not only did they agree, but they pushed the transplant team to find a place for his heart. The team wasn't sure they could find a baby close enough to receive their son's heart, but then they found the baby in Birmingham and rushed the organ for surgery.

My heart hurts for that family. I can't imagine losing a child in any manner. But my heart also swells with admiration in the Christ-like action, their determination to help others even in the midst of their suffering. Their decision saved another child's life, blessed another family… and reminded many people, like myself, of what it truly means to live like Christ.

This Week: Search online for stories of organ donations touching lives and remind yourself of how, in a world filled with pain and suffering, there are those who push through the pain and find that some of the most amazing gifts can be given—and received—in the midst of a storm.

MY PRAYER TO START THIS WEEK:

_____

_____

_____

_____

_____

THOSE TO REMEMBER IN PRAYER THIS WEEK:

_____

_____

_____

_____

_____

_____

_____

MONDAY, MARCH 13

"WHEN THEY KEPT ON QUESTIONING *him, he straightened up and said to them, "Let any one of you who is without sin be the first to throw a stone at her." John 8:7*

(Written by our oldest son, Rene Zeringue, regarding a conversation with our preacher, Wayne Dunaway. This was too good not to share.)

Brother Wayne said something yesterday that I will hold onto for a long time. He said, "Drop the stones, and pass the bread." He was teaching from John 8 when the scribes bring the woman caught in the act of adultery to Jesus and ask him what to do with her. Of course you know the story, Jesus bends and writes something in the sand; many think that Jesus was writing the sexual sins of the men that were standing there before him. He then stood and said, "Let anyone who has not sinned cast the first stone." After they had each left, oldest to youngest, he turns to the woman and, with love, says, "Where are your accusers, has no one condemned you?" She answers, "They are gone." He responds, "Then neither do I condemn you, go and sin no more."

What Christ does is show these scribes (what they already knew) that they too deserved to be stoned for their sins, so if they were going to condemn her for it, they were going down with her.

Here is what is absolutely beautiful about Christianity: we Christians are not the religious people that stand with stones in our hands waiting to throw them at the woman caught in sin; we ARE the woman that has stood before Christ, guilty, deserving of death, to which Christ said, "I do not condemn you. Go and sin no more." We are the woman who has FELT the GRACE and LOVE of the one true King that we sinned against. We do not throw stones at the lost precisely because WE WERE

THEM, AND STILL ARE THEM in that we still DESERVE to be stoned, but Christ has let us off only because of His grace and love for us.

When we gather around the communion table, we are passing the bread and fruit of the vine to liars, cheaters, adulterers, idolaters, all that deserved to be stoned, but were forgiven and made perfect by Christ.

Because of this, when we see those caught in the snares of the world and of sin, our response shouldn't be to grab a stone, but to pass the bread.

This Week: Undoubtedly, you have someone in your life who has sinned against you or a loved one. Though it is difficult, follow Christ's example here—drop the stones, and pass the bread.

MY PRAYER TO START THIS WEEK:

_____

_____

_____

_____

_____

THOSE TO REMEMBER IN PRAYER THIS WEEK:

_____

_____

_____

_____

_____

_____

_____

MONDAY, MARCH 20

"REJOICE ALWAYS, PRAY CONTINUALLY, GIVE *thanks in all circumstances; for this is God's will for you in Christ Jesus.*" *1 Thessalonians 5:16-18*

As a teen, I wasn't the best at being thankful. In fact, I was far from it. My parents both worked hard to give us everything we needed. My father built tires at the Goodyear plant; my mother sewed infant clothes at the Health-Tex plant. I didn't know any of my friends' parents who, in my opinion, worked harder than mine. But in spite of my parents sacrificing to attempt to give us everything we needed/wanted, I wasn't as appreciative as I should have been. I would eye my friends' new clothes, their jewelry, new cars with a green eye. Even things as trivial as the newest makeups caused a bitter vein of jealousy to find its way to my heart.

When I turned sixteen, I honestly didn't expect to receive a car. And my parents weren't able to buy one; however, they had Daddy's 1973 Buick Century repainted and fixed up so that I, like the majority of the other kids in my grade, would have a vehicle to drive to school. Now, don't get me wrong; I was thrilled to have a car to drive. BUT—I was still envious of the new Camaro that a friend drove each morning and parked in her spot, right next to mine. Ditto for the Corvette and Firebird a few parking spaces down.

But then, one of the football players stopped me and asked if he and some of the other teammates could take a look under the hood (to be honest, I didn't even know how to open the hood then, but they helped). They marveled at how well the engine had been maintained and cleaned. And they all but drooled over the 350 engine, with several asking if they could drive it sometime.

Suddenly, I had the "cool" car. And my appreciation for my parents' gift went through the roof. This was no longer my Daddy's old work car; it was my treasure! I made sure to keep it clean, was happy to open the hood to the people that asked (and many did) and was absolutely joyful that I had such an amazing ride.

Thinking about me back then, and the way I felt when I saw my car through another's eyes, I wonder if, when people see Christians, they see us as something that isn't desirable, something old and not as shiny as the world, with its appealing sin. In fact, the only way they may have to see the beauty of the gift is if they see it through my eyes, the way I finally saw the splendor of my car through the football team's eyes. Perhaps, if I really want to bring others to Christ, I need to make sure that they see enough appealing about the way I'm living my life…that they want to look inside and see more. I hope, when they do, that they are as excited as those guys were when they found that 350 under the hood.

This Week: If you 'wake up on the wrong side of the bed,' remember that someone may be watching you today and seeing what Christ looks like through you. Even though you may be going through a rough spot right now, think of five things to be thankful for. Recall those blessings throughout the day so that others will want to know more about what you have inside, the way those guys wanted to know what was hiding inside of my 'old' Buick!

MY PRAYER TO START THIS WEEK:

_____

_____

_____

_____

_____

THOSE TO REMEMBER IN PRAYER THIS WEEK:

_____

_____

_____

_____

_____

_____

_____

MONDAY, MARCH 27

"WHEN TEMPTED, NO ONE SHOULD *say, "God is tempting me."* *For God cannot be tempted by evil, nor does he tempt anyone; but each person is tempted when they are dragged away by their own evil desire and enticed. Then, after desire has conceived, it gives birth to sin; and sin, when it is full-grown, gives birth to death." James 1:13-15*

As everyone in the room snickered, I watched our oldest son, Rene, ask our oldest grandson, Alanus, the same question.

"You *didn't* eat a doughnut?"

Alanus, eyes wide, shook his head again. "No, sir."

What Alanus didn't know, and what had the whole room struggling to contain the laughter, was that his right cheek was covered in white sugar from the doughnuts on the platter. The same doughnuts he'd been told he couldn't eat.

As Rene looked to all of the adults in the room in disbelief, one of the kids who had been watching Alanus explained, "He didn't eat one. He just moved them on the plate and then licked his fingers."

Temptation. It's so tough to resist, and often, we get close enough to the forbidden fruit…that we look guilty, merely because we've gotten too close, like my grandson and that tray of doughnuts.

I have no doubt that, if left alone with that plate, eventually moving the doughnuts around and licking his fingers wouldn't have been enough. The temptation would've been too strong, and he'd have given in. Like-wise, when I know I struggle with something tempting, I'm only hurting myself by getting closer to the situation, or to the thing I want so badly, or to the individual who isn't good for my spiritual life.

Now, I'm not saying that I stay away from those that I might have the opportunity to bring to God; however, I also need to remind myself that, if a person—or thing—is keeping me from Him, then I need to get away from the plate...before I'm standing, ashamed, with sugar on my cheek.

This Week: Take inventory of your biggest temptations. I'm assuming everyone has more than one; I know I do. If you've placed yourself in a situation that is setting you up to fail, back away. Ask for help from a family member or friend—even better if you know someone who struggles with the same problem—and keep yourself from standing in front of your Father with sugar on your cheek.

MY PRAYER TO START THIS WEEK:

_____

_____

_____

_____

_____

THOSE TO REMEMBER IN PRAYER THIS WEEK:

_____

_____

_____

_____

_____

_____

_____

_____

MONDAY, APRIL 3

"THEREFORE, MY DEAR BROTHERS AND *sisters, stand firm. Let nothing move you. Always give yourselves fully to the work of the Lord, because you know that your labor in the Lord is not in vain."* 1 Corinthians 15:58

We lived in Atlanta from 1994-2000 and attended a fabulous church there during that time. We hadn't attended a church that sang a lot of the contemporary praise songs before, and this one introduced us to many that we still love. The worship leader would also prompt you to think more about the words and the meaning. For example, whenever we sang "I Stand in Awe," the congregation would begin singing while seated… but when we got to the chorus, we would all stand. It was so moving and powerful to stand and raise our voices together in awe of our Lord.

Fast-forward to 2001. We had moved to North Alabama and attended a much smaller church that had just started singing the songs that we'd come to love in Atlanta. And on that very first Sunday, the church sang, "I Stand in Awe." Naturally, when the chorus started, J.R. and I stood and continued singing.

And it didn't take us but a second to realize…

We were the only ones standing.

Now, let me tell you a little about the people around us. Many of them were people I had attended church with for years during my youth. Several were my relatives. In fact, my sister nudged my brother-in-law to stand so that we weren't on our own, but he shook his head. And she remained in her pew as well. It was just out of the comfort zone for everyone in the building, and no one was budging.

In spite of this awkward fact, J.R. and I remained standing through the remainder of the song, and then sat with the rest of the congregation.

I think about that first service at our small church often, particularly when I encounter other situations in life where I feel I'm standing on my own. Every now and then, when we follow our Savior, it causes us to stand out from the crowd, to feel different, even a bit awkward. And we have a choice. We can sit back down and blend in with the masses, or we can remain standing, unashamed, and praising our Heavenly Father.

I'd love to say I always remain standing, the way my husband and I did that Sunday at our new church, but sometimes the awkwardness gets the best of me, and I disappear within the crowd instead of standing tall for my Lord. But Christ stood up for me, didn't He? *He went to the cross for me!* And I pray for His forgiveness when I find myself quietly blending instead of standing for His glory.

This Week: When you are tempted to take the easy route, to blend with the masses instead of standing against the crowd, remember the One who stood for you, who still stands for you and who will always stand for you. And make a difference. Do not be afraid to be seen. Oh, and about that small congregation in Alabama…they still sing "I Stand in Awe" fairly often. But nowadays, when they hit the chorus…everyone stands. ☺

MY PRAYER TO START THIS WEEK:

_____

_____

_____

_____

_____

THOSE TO REMEMBER IN PRAYER THIS WEEK:

_____

_____

_____

_____

_____

_____

MONDAY, APRIL 10

"BE ALERT AND OF SOBER *mind. Your enemy the devil prowls around like a roaring lion looking for someone to devour." I Peter 5:8*

"I see a snake."

Now, that isn't a sentence that I would typically type without an exclamation point at the end, but in this case, that's exactly how our oldest grandson made the statement. Therefore, I presumed he was either kidding or knew that what he saw was actually a stick. There were quite a few tree limbs extending from the water at the river, and I'd noticed some were even curved to appear rather snake-like.

I grinned at J.R, said we should probably go see what he was talking about, and casually walked toward the river's edge, where Alanus stood, pointing toward the water.

Sure enough, as we peered over the edge, the snake lifted his head above the surface.

I screamed, and then looked at the proximity of the snake to where Alanus had been in the water merely seconds ago. He'd been less than five feet from the thing. "Alanus," I said, "that is *not* how you act when you see a snake. When you see a snake, you do this." And I ran, screaming, to the house, while he and our other grandchildren laughed.

That snake didn't hurt anyone that day, but it reminded me of the serpent we learn about in Genesis, the one who is still so prevalent. In the verse above, the devil is described as a roaring lion, prowling as he looks for someone to devour. But, like that snake lurking in the water, the devil can sometimes wait quietly, patiently. And if we aren't watching for him, we might not see him until it is too late, and we've gotten too close, close enough for him to strike.

Likewise, when we do see the signs that the devil is trying to have his way with us, or with our friends or family, we should take note in the differences in the way Alanus and I handled seeing that snake. If we make a subdued statement—"I see a snake,"—no one is likely to take us seriously, in the same way my husband and I didn't think our grandson was serious. But if we alert others, pointing out the dangers and fleeing from sin, kicking and screaming, then they will undoubtedly pay attention… and also turn away.

This Week: If you sense yourself, a friend or loved one getting too close to danger, something that could harm them, don't remain silent. You may be saving their life or, more importantly, their soul.

MY PRAYER TO START THIS WEEK:

_____

_____

_____

_____

_____

THOSE TO REMEMBER IN PRAYER THIS WEEK:

_____

_____

_____

_____

_____

_____

_____

MONDAY, APRIL 17

" A HAPPY HEART MAKES THE FACE *cheerful, but heartache crushes the spirit." Proverbs 15:13*

In the mid 1990s, I worked for a year as a paraprofessional (parapro) in the Special Needs classroom at my children's school in Georgia. At the time, my husband traveled nearly every week and spent months working overseas. We had three foster children we were trying to adopt, and all of them had special needs, so I grew close to the other special needs children at the school and spent a good deal of time in the classroom. Eventually, I was offered a job to actually get paid for my time spent at the school.

I'd never planned to work as a parapro, hadn't known all that much about working with special needs children until I had three of my own. But that was one of the most rewarding experiences of my life. First, because I met teachers who went above and beyond the call of duty each day taking care of children who truly needed supervision twenty-four/seven. And second, because these children would grab my heart and hold it, so that even now, I feel a tug in my chest at the memory of my time spent with them.

One little boy in the class had been deprived of oxygen after birth and had an abundance of difficulties as a result. He couldn't walk or crawl, couldn't talk, couldn't feed himself or use the bathroom on his own. But, as I soon learned after working with him, he could laugh. And not a soft chuckle or giggle, but a full-throated, toss his head back and burst forward kind of laugh that never failed to pull a smile from everyone around, even on the worst of days.

But one of the unique aspects of his disability was that his brain had a delayed reaction to stimuli. And because of this, when he would see or hear something funny, he would appear stoic for a short time, usually a few minutes, so that the moment would pass, and the classroom curriculum would have us moving on to another topic.

And then he would laugh. And laugh. And laugh.

Which, of course, would have us replaying the events of the preceding minutes until we recalled what he would find funny.

Nowadays, when I think about him and about those outbursts of laughter and the puzzle of determining the cause each time, I consider how his delayed reaction is indicative of our influence on others as we live our Christian lives. We're going along, doing our best to be Christ-like, and yet it seems there is no response. We are met with stoicism. Apathy.

Or so it seems.

What we may not know, or may never see, is the delayed reaction when that individual recalls our actions…and smiles. Or, like that precious little boy, tosses his head back and laughs.

Maybe the response will have nothing to do with laughter, but in a spirit that is touched, and a heart that finds itself yearning for the One that they saw reflected in your actions.

This Week: Call your local school and ask if they have a special needs program. Offer to volunteer as a reader in the classroom. Experience the beauty of helping those that can't always help themselves.

MY PRAYER TO START THIS WEEK:

_____

_____

_____

_____

_____

THOSE TO REMEMBER IN PRAYER THIS WEEK:

_____

_____

_____

_____

_____

_____

MONDAY, APRIL 24

" AH, SOVEREIGN LORD, YOU HAVE *made the heavens and the earth by your great power and outstretched arm. Nothing is too hard for you."*
Jeremiah 32:17

I've been praying. No, that isn't all that unusual. I do my best to pray daily, and I strive to pray more than the initial prayer time J.R. and I share each morning to begin our day and the mealtime blessings. But lately, I've had something on my heart that is simply causing me to follow 1 Thessalonians 5:17's directive to pray continually.

Have you ever found yourself like that? So wrapped up in something, absorbed in it, consumed by it, or—as in my case now—distraught over it, that you simply can't stop praying? That's where I am.

If you follow me on social media or have read my devotions in the past, you know I'm a kidney donor. I can't say enough about the joy of giving a chance at a normal life to someone, and in my case, the young man who was a stranger on the day we met and I decided to donate my kidney to him…but is now part of my family. He's like a son. And when he hurts, I hurt.

So when he called to tearfully tell me that he was in the hospital and that the kidney wasn't working correctly, I hurt. And I prayed. It's been five years since our transplant, and the kidney has done fine. Matt has been living a normal life with no dialysis. He has been able to take trips with his family. He has had two sons. At the time that I write this, Ryan is close to turning three and Brooks will have his first birthday the same month as his big brother.

I've been praying. Praying that my kidney won't fail. Praying that Matt will continue to live a normal life. Praying that I can be a very real part of his life, because a part of me lives in him. But, in the midst of all of this praying, I found myself saying…

"God, if You can, heal Matt."

If You can? How *dare* I *question* my Lord? The God that created the universe can do anything He pleases (Psalm 115:3 and 135:6). Didn't I pay attention to those powerful verses in Job 38, when Job dared to question God?

I've been praying. Usually, prayer makes me stronger, but at other times, like now, my prayers show me just how weak I am…without my Lord. Yes, He can heal Matt. He can move mountains. He can create. He can destroy. He is the Almighty. And He is my Lord.

And I trust Him.

I've been praying. Praying continually. Praying that Matt will be okay and praying that I will be okay too, that I will keep my faith strong and trust God's plan. Most of all, I've been praying…for God's will to be done. If the medical team can't cause my kidney to work as it should, and if Matt ends up on dialysis again, it isn't because God didn't answer my prayers. It isn't because He can't do anything He pleases. It is because that was not my Lord's will. And I will trust His will. Always. Forever.

Forgive me, Lord.

This Week: Are you praying continually over a piercing struggle? Are you or someone you love going through a difficult time physically? Emotionally? Spiritually? Do you have a loved one at death's door? Does your heart ache, and you feel certain no one understands? Trust this: God does. And believe this, whether your request is answered with a yes or a no, trust in Him, that He knows your heartaches and, whether the outcome is your utmost desire—or your biggest heartache—God's will be done.

MY PRAYER TO START THIS WEEK:

_____

_____

_____

_____

_____

THOSE TO REMEMBER IN PRAYER THIS WEEK:

_____

_____

_____

_____

_____

_____

_____

MONDAY, MAY 1

"WE LOVE BECAUSE HE FIRST *loved us.*" *1 John 4:19*

(Written by our oldest son, Rene Zeringue.)

My daughter doesn't love me. I know that sounds like the opening statement of a man lying on a couch in front of a PhD, but the statement remains. She doesn't love me. Granted: she is not yet a month old. She does not yet comprehend love, nor will she for at least another . . . 20 years or so. She is still figuring out what is going on in this bright place. Her eyes are deep, yet shallow. She does not love me, but she will. I don't know when it will begin, I don't know how it will start, but I do know that it will happen. Why will it happen, you ask? Because I love her. I love her now. Right now. Before she loves me, I love her. Because I hold her, because I kiss her incessantly, because I express my love throughout each day, because I provide for her, because I care in a way unknown before my sons arrived, because I love her now, she will love me. I long for that day with everything in me. It is going to bring me untold joy each time I hear it, as it does now with my sons.

Praise God that He loved you first. When you had not even begun to comprehend love, when you were still figuring out this bright place, when your eyes were shallow, when you did not love Him, He loved you. God longed for the day with everything in Him that you would reciprocate that love, and it brings Him untold joy each time He hears and sees it. Praise God that He loved you first.

Isaiah 64:7 – "There is no one who calls upon your name, who rouses himself to take hold of you; for you have hidden your face from us, and have made us melt in the hand of our iniquities."

Romans 3:10-12 – "No one seeks for God."

They are telling me that we are not too far away from my daughter reaching for me. She has not done that yet, but she will. I reach for her now. Many, many times each day, I reach for her. I reach for her to change her, to burp her, to carry her from place to place, to comfort her, but most times I reach for her just to hold her, to have her closer to me, to love her. I reach for her again and again, and because I do, she will reach for me one day, and I cannot wait. Again, I long for that day with everything in me.

Praise God that He reached for you first. When you were not only unable to reach but unwilling, he reached for you. When you were convinced that you were good on your own, that you did not need help, that you were sufficient, he reached for you. When you were convinced that you had all of the answers you needed, He reached for you. When you did nothing but cry and whine with all selfishness, He reached for you. WHAT JOY it brought Him the day you reached for Him, because He first reached for you. WHAT JOY it brings Him each day as you reach, arms to the Heavens, for the One that you love. Praise God that He reached for you first.

This Week: The next time you see a baby, their eyes attempting to focus and see you, their faces confused and attempting to learn about this great big world surrounding them…think about the fact that, even when you couldn't comprehend the mere essence of love, when you were simply something to be cared for…He reached for you. He cared for you. He loved you! Praise God!

MY PRAYER TO START THIS WEEK:

_____

_____

_____

_____

_____

THOSE TO REMEMBER IN PRAYER THIS WEEK:

_____

_____

_____

_____

_____

_____

_____

MONDAY, MAY 8

" **I**LONG TO SEE YOU SO *that I may impart to you some spiritual gift to make you strong—that is, that you and I may be mutually encouraged by each other's faith." Romans 1:11-12*

If I had to choose my favorite family vacations, I wouldn't list those where we stayed in a hotel or had someone preparing our meals or making our beds. In fact, I'd probably choose the trips that involve the most work, our treasured camping trips.

Camping? Treasured?

Yes. And yes.

Ever since our boys were little, we've had family camping trips, as well as camping trips that involved groups of friends, often our friends from church. We typically arrive in the evening, pitch our tents and then find ourselves lulled to sleep by crickets, owls and frogs. Since most of our camping locations are away from any type of town, the sky is pitch black…except for those magnificent stars. All of God's creation just seems more vivid, more real, when you get away from the hustle of the world and take a chance to breathe.

On these trips, our days are filled with children riding bicycles, running and playing around a campground. Afternoons and evenings find us all cooking together, then sitting around a campfire where we chat and laugh and sing. We roast hot dogs and marshmallows over an open fire (marshmallows are inevitably nestled against a chunk of chocolate and placed between two graham crackers for s'mores).

Because we've moved several times over the years, the friends that accompany us on our camping trips have changed due to proximity. However, the families that have shared those special times with us are still some of our closest friends today. There's something to be said for encouraging each other's faith together, particularly when you are doing something that reminds you of your Lord.

And, perhaps because God is so clearly on display during these precious times, conversations often center around Him, around our faith and around our appreciation toward our Creator.

Are you wanting to take a camping trip yet? I know I am.

Why are those vacations so much more memorable than the ones where we were waited on hand and foot?

Because of the fellowship. The time spent *together* enjoying each other's company. The meals created *together* and then consumed *together*. The joy of marveling over God's creation…*together*. It is as if we're glimpsing heaven. And it makes me look forward to that amazing fellowship we'll experience there, with our Lord!

This Week: Plan a camping trip. Invite some friends and enjoy the beauty of God's world and the fellowship of God's people.

MY PRAYER TO START THIS WEEK:

_____

_____

_____

_____

_____

_____

THOSE TO REMEMBER IN PRAYER THIS WEEK:

_____

_____

_____

_____

_____

_____

_____

MONDAY, MAY 15

" ENTER THROUGH THE NARROW GATE. *For wide is the gate and broad is the road that leads to destruction, and many enter through it. But small is the gate and narrow the road that leads to life, and only a few find it.*" *Matthew 7:13-14*

I've mentioned how much we love to camp, and when we camp, we also enjoy hiking, especially when those hikes allow us to see things that we would miss when traveling by car or motorcycle.

If you've ever traveled the mountains of North Georgia, you've probably heard about the abundance of hiking trails in the area. You may have even driven past the signs that noted a trail path nearby. If you did drive past, you missed out, especially if the trail ended with one of the natural waterfalls the area is known for.

On one of our camping trips near Helen, Georgia, J.R. and I decided to take the boys hiking to see as many waterfalls as possible during our stay. We would get up early in the morning, drive to the point where the trail began and then start the journey.

We had been told about one particularly difficult hike. "It's a tough one, but the end is so worth the journey." Unfortunately, we decided to save this particular hike until our last day, and on that day, the forecast called for rain.

Determined to see the breathtaking waterfall that everyone had told us about, we started down the path. And as we'd been told, the trail grew very narrow at times, to where we had to walk single-file along a ledge. At other times, the trees seemed to crowd us in, causing the forest floor to darken from their shade and making the hike seem more frightening than exciting. Sure enough, when we were about halfway there, and in the thickest part of the woods, it began to rain.

We found shelter in a shallow cave while waiting for the storm to pass. J.R. and I had brought backpacks with water and snacks for the boys (they were still fairly young at this time) and attempted to make the snag in our plan as enjoyable as possible. Typical boys, they thought the time in the cave made the day even more "cool."

Finally, the rain passed, and we had a decision to make: do we turn around and give up on seeing this waterfall, or do we continue, even though the skies were still churning, another storm potentially brewing to hit us as we made the trek.

With a bit of trepidation on my part, we decided to carry on. The rain carried on too, causing us to slide on slippery rocks and tumble on tree roots or slick leaves.

Toward the end of the journey, we were all drenched. And cold. And weary. But then…the sun began to shine. And we heard the thundering rush of water up ahead. Pushing forward through the final batch of trees, we saw what all the fuss was about.

Have mercy, it was amazing. And so very well worth the journey. Water burst forward, cascading and pounding and splashing its way down the mountain, soaking us even more, but this was different. This wasn't the dark rain trying to keep us from making the trip but this was the reward, a refreshing splash reminding us that we'd survived the terrain and had been awarded one of the most exquisite scenes I'd ever witnessed.

The path was narrow. The ground was rocky and tough. We were wet. And cold. And tired.

Isn't that how we feel sometimes in life? Wouldn't it be easier to turn around and take the easy route? To forget about the breathtaking glory that awaits at the end of the journey? But oh, what we would've missed if we'd have turned around. And didn't it seem even sweeter…because of the difficult terrain?

This Week: Search and find the nearest waterfall. Hike to see that stunning creation of God. Thank Him for that view…and for the journey you took to see it. Then thank Him for the ultimate reward at the end of life's journey.

MY PRAYER TO START THIS WEEK:

_____

_____

_____

_____

_____

_____

THOSE TO REMEMBER IN PRAYER THIS WEEK:

_____

_____

_____

_____

_____

_____

_____

MONDAY, MAY 22

" BUT WHILE HE WAS STILL *a long way off, his father saw him and was filled with compassion for him; he ran to his son, threw his arms around him and kissed him."* Luke 15:20

I grew up in a small town in North Alabama—Glencoe—population roughly 5,000. Small enough that everyone knows pretty much everyone, that there are only a couple of traffic lights needed, and that you can take a few blinks while driving through…and miss the town completely.

For the first twenty years of my life, I dreamed of moving away, living in a big city, meeting new people, experiencing exciting things that could never be accomplished in my tiny town.

Or so I thought.

For the second twenty years of my life, I lived in many cities. I started in New Orleans (quite a contrast from Glencoe, to say the least), moved to Huntsville, Tuscaloosa, Atlanta, and a few other places in between. I lived in the big cities. I met new people. I experienced exciting things that couldn't be accomplished in my hometown.

Then…I moved back home.

And I started noticing things that I hadn't appreciated before, the beauty of small-town living, where you have relationships with people who not only know you, but they also know your parents, your siblings, your history. The neighborhoods where no one passes by without waving. The friendliness of the people at the local grocery, where it isn't a rush to see how quickly you can move your cart through the aisles, but a tradition of visiting with friends also shopping.

This past weekend, we moved into a house in the very neighborhood where I grew up. This morning, I walked down the street to pay my water bill (yes, I can do that here), and I passed beneath the canopy of trees where I often walked with my Granny. I remembered her slow and steady gait and the way she would point out the gardens and what vegetables were growing, the pastures of cattle and horses, the bits of God's creation that she appreciated each day. And what I appreciate now that I am back and older and…wiser.

Wiser as to what is important. Wiser as to how the less hectic life isn't all that bad. In fact, I prefer it. And wiser in knowing that this, being nearer to my family (my parents and both of our sons live in this neighborhood too) and back near my roots, is as close to heaven as I can get on earth.

The only things missing…are the loved ones who've gone on to their reward. And when I see them again, then, I'll truly be home.

This Week: Spend some time looking at photos of your youth, at the original place you called "home". If possible, visit it again, or hey, do what I did, and move back! Think about how amazing it will be when you are really…home.

MY PRAYER TO START THIS WEEK:

_____

_____

_____

_____

_____

_____

THOSE TO REMEMBER IN PRAYER THIS WEEK:

_____

_____

_____

_____

_____

_____

_____

MONDAY, MAY 29

"SO WHOEVER KNOWS THE RIGHT *thing to do and fails to do it, for him it is sin." James 4:17*

Recently, J.R. took our van through a car wash beside one of the local gas station. We'd taken the van through the wash several times before, but this time, one of the swirling brushes along the side caught our passenger mirror and ripped it off, causing it to shatter as it slammed again and again against the car door.

I wasn't with J.R. when he went through the car wash, but later, as we drove the van, he explained what had happened that caused the mirror to be broken.

Now, I could have nodded, told him that was terrible and continued about my day…as though I didn't know more about the broken mirror than I was letting on. But, even though J.R. had no way of knowing, that wouldn't have been the right thing to do.

So, I confessed.

I said, "The truth is, *I* hit a mailbox as I left the neighborhood last week. The mirror fell off, and I stuck it back on. Apparently, I didn't stick it on as well as I thought."

As I suspected, he started to laugh. And then we both laughed. It was pretty funny, after all. Not so much that I hit a mailbox, but that I thought I had "fixed" it by sticking the mirror back into place.

Confession. Sometimes, like when I admitted to hitting the mailbox, confession isn't all that difficult. Other times, however, it's downright painful. No one wants to admit when they've done wrong, especially if whatever they did affected others. But, as the verse states above, if we know the right thing to do and do not do it, that is sin. And it is by confessing our sins that we have our forgiven and are cleansed from all unrighteousness (1 John 1:9).

True, most things I need to confess are much more substantial than my mirror hitting a mailbox, but the principle remains the same. God wants me to do the right thing, and whether that means something as small as telling my husband I hit a mailbox…or as big as hurting a loved one, I need to do the right thing.

This Week: If someone has confessed a sin toward you, do as God would have you to do; forgive them.

MY PRAYER TO START THIS WEEK:

_____

_____

_____

_____

_____

THOSE TO REMEMBER IN PRAYER THIS WEEK:

_____

_____

_____

_____

_____

_____

_____

_____

MONDAY, JUNE 5

"BUT THE LORD SAID TO *Samuel, "Do not consider his appearance or his height, for I have rejected him. The Lord does not look at the things people look at. People look at the outward appearance, but the Lord looks at the heart."* 1 Samuel 16:7

As we sat in the waiting room for labor and delivery, I listened to a woman sharing the news of her grandchild's birth on the phone.

"He has ten fingers and ten toes. He's absolutely perfect!"

I glanced to J.R., sitting beside me, and then to the other family members sitting with us and waiting for the birth of our third grandson. I know J.R. heard the comment and thought the same thing I did, but I am not certain whether our other family members heard the statement, and I didn't point it out at the time.

Everyone was very sensitive to the topic then, because our grandson had yet to be born; however, from the ultrasounds that had occurred in the preceding months, we knew that he was missing at least one digit on his right hand. Now, I know the lady wouldn't have ever made the statement if she had known, but even so, it stung.

Her grandson was absolutely perfect, she said. But all I could think was…

So is ours.

Ten fingers and ten toes doesn't equate to perfection. In fact, one of our dearest friends was born without arms. But when I look at Mr. Dean, I don't think about his disability. And when I look at our grandson Ryan, now three years old and thriving, I don't even notice the difference in his fingers. He's adjusted very well and uses both hands fine, even hitting a baseball on one of our recent trips to see him in Tennessee. But the main reason I don't notice anything different with both of them is because I'm not looking at the outward appearance. I look at them…and feel love. I look at them…and see their hearts.

This Week: In everyone you meet this week, look beyond the superficial and see the real person beneath. Look at others the way God looks at us, so that you aren't noticing anything…but the heart.

MY PRAYER TO START THIS WEEK:

_____

_____

_____

_____

_____

_____

THOSE TO REMEMBER IN PRAYER THIS WEEK:

_____

_____

_____

_____

_____

_____

_____

MONDAY, JUNE 12

"WE LOVE BECAUSE HE FIRST *loved us.*" *1 John 4:19*

(Written by our youngest son, Kaleb Zeringue.)

Thursdays are my weekly marathon. I wake up, drive to Birmingham, spend a few hours there, drive straight back to Gadsden (an hour one way) to eat lunch and then head to the gym and coach until it's dark outside. Then I head home and rest.

The past two weeks I have had new motivation and anticipation for arriving back home. It's this little guy, Konrad Asher Zeringue, born June 8th.

What has he done to warrant such affection? To capture my thoughts and imagination all day on my busiest of days?

He has pooped on himself, every day since I met him, peed on me countless times, grunted so loudly in his sleep that he wakes me and his mom up. He really likes to grunt. He also throws both of his arms up when he sleeps, cries for me and his mom when we are right next to him, stares at me blankly as I desperately try to be the first one to make him laugh, makes hilarious faces when he sees sunlight and, most importantly, he's MY SON.

Such is the way with God, I think. We try so hard to impress God and earn his love and affection, but all the while, we are pooping everywhere, grunting in our sleep, crying when we don't feel Him or hear His voice (even when He is right next to us), and looking at Him blankly when we don't understand Him.

Konrad has not earned my affection, yet he has all of my affection and favor and love because *he is my son*. In the same way, you and I have not earned God's love, but we have ALL of His affection and ALL of His Favor and ALL of His love...because we are His Sons and Daughters through the holy adoption that took place when Christ went to the cross and died for us.

This Week: If you have a baby in your home, pay attention to how many times he or she needs you on a daily basis. If you don't, offer to babysit for a friend, so you can be reminded of how needy that little person is. Then imagine yourself as God sees you...as a child needing our heavenly Father. Praise God that He loves us even when we're as needy and as messy as that precious (and sometimes needy and messy) bundle of joy!

MY PRAYER TO START THIS WEEK:

_____

_____

_____

_____

_____

THOSE TO REMEMBER IN PRAYER THIS WEEK:

_____

_____

_____

_____

_____

_____

_____

MONDAY, JUNE 19

"BE STRONG AND COURAGEOUS. DO *not be afraid; do not be discouraged, for the Lord your God will be with you wherever you go."* *Joshua 1:9*

One of our employees needed help with her move from Florida to Alabama, so J.R. and I helped her load the moving van. Afterwards, J.R. needed to go to work, and she needed me to drive the car so she could drive the moving truck. Now, this wasn't some old battered vehicle; it wasn't even a month old. I was nervous about driving the new vehicle, but she assured me that she didn't mind me driving her new car and was actually grateful to have someone to drive it.

So I started driving the car, which happened to be a hybrid. When I reached the first red light, I noticed the brake pedal seemed to work differently than what I was used to. But I assumed this had to do with the new car and the fact that it was a hybrid. I wasn't too concerned and, when the light turned green, I turned onto the interstate.

A few miles down the road, I noticed the pedal still didn't seem to work the way it should. But again, I thought it was the car. Then my phone rang. She had locked herself out of the moving truck, and the extra set of keys was in her car. The car I was driving.

I turned around at the next exit and started heading back. By the time I exited the interstate, the brake pedal wouldn't stop before hitting the floor. I knew something was wrong but, from the place I was in the center of a six-lane road, I had no choice but to try to get to her apartment, a block away. I drove as slow as possible, put on the flashers and prayed that God would get me back safely.

Finally, I pulled into the parking lot at her apartment complex and allowed the car to roll to a stop near her apartment. I told her what had happened, and we called AAA. When the serviceman arrived, he informed us that the brakes were not working at all. If I'd have continued driving on the busy interstate, I would most assuredly have had an accident and could have hurt someone else if the car would have crashed into another vehicle.

I knew God had heard my prayers. And I believe He set all of the odd series of events in order. He put me in the right place to be the one she would ask to drive the car, instead of having someone probably much younger behind the wheel (experience does help with driving, of course, and I've got several more years of experience than her young friends). He knew she would lock her keys in her car. He knew she would call me at the precise moment that she needed to for me to turn around and make it back safely to her apartment. He knew that we would determine what was wrong…without me crashing into someone else or without one of her friends trying to drive the car to Alabama and having an accident along the way.

He was with us. I have no doubt. He kept both of us safe. And even if a crash would have occurred (I have had some wrecks in the past—not recently, but in my younger years), then I know that He would have also been with us.

He is always with us, in the good times and in the bad. Watching over us and keeping watch over us…until He calls us home.

This Week: Think of the last time that everything happened at precisely the right time to keep you out of harm's way. Know that God was there, and that He is always there.

MY PRAYER TO START THIS WEEK:

_____

_____

_____

_____

_____

THOSE TO REMEMBER IN PRAYER THIS WEEK:

_____

_____

_____

_____

_____

_____

_____

MONDAY, JUNE 26

"WHEN JESUS REACHED THE SPOT, *he looked up and said to him,* *"Zacchaeus, come down immediately. I must stay at your house today."* Luke 19:5

Isn't it amazing how good it feels to be recognized by someone important? Can you think of a time when someone you looked up to or admired recognized you? Actually called you by name?

Our youngest son Kaleb recently spoke about a time when he was little, only four years old, when he was recognized by someone famous. Though he didn't call Kaleb by name, the moment was so prominent in our son's life that even now, twenty-one years later, he still recalls the way he felt.

We were at a Braves game and had bought our tickets far enough ahead that we had really good seats, about seven rows behind the area where the Braves players took their practice swings. Chipper Jones was up to bat, and he fouled off a ball that landed near Brian Jordan, currently taking his practice swings.

Brian Jordan picked up the ball and turned toward the crowd, where little boys who were familiar with what would happen hustled toward the bottom row in the hopes that he would hand them the coveted ball. This was Rene and Kaleb's first time to attend a game, so they were a little shy about going forward, even with JR and I nudging them and encouraging them. Kaleb, our youngest, was most definitely the smallest child attempting to move toward the baseball player, with other kids pushing ahead of him.

Brian Jordan scanned the group, spotted Kaleb near the back and motioned for him to come forward. He then gave Kaleb the ball.

And to this day, Kaleb says Brian Jordan is his favorite baseball player. The famous guy became even more famous in my child's eyes, because he noticed him, acknowledged him, showed him favor.

Imagine how Zaccheus felt that day, when he was noticed, acknowledged and shown favor by his Lord. And imagine how amazing it will feel for us one day when we enter the gates of heaven to find ourselves noticed, acknowledged and shown favor by our Savior and King.

This Week: Follow Christ's example. Notice, acknowledge and show favor to someone who isn't expecting it. Treat others as Christ would treat them, and as He would treat you.

MY PRAYER TO START THIS WEEK:

_____

_____

_____

_____

_____

THOSE TO REMEMBER IN PRAYER THIS WEEK:

_____

_____

_____

_____

_____

_____

_____

MONDAY, JULY 3

" SAVE ME, O GOD, FOR *the waters have come up to my neck. I sink in the miry depths, where there is no foothold. I have come into the deep waters; the floods engulf me." Galatians 6:10*

My sister and I had taken all of our children to a swimming pond about a half hour from our home. At the time, we had four little boys (my niece was born shortly after). Typical little boys, they were always getting into something, and this day was no exception.

We rented a pedal boat and took the four boys out into the water. Gina and I were pedaling and enjoying the beautiful day, and we thought the boys were enjoying the ride in the back. Consequently, we had six people in a five-person pedal boat, which didn't seem to be a problem, since the boys were all pretty small. But that was before my nephew Mason found something to do to entertain himself in the back.

By the time we reached the center of the pond, a loud voice boomed out over the water (I had never realized the place had speakers in the trees until now, because no one had ever had a reason to call out to us before). And the voice said…

"Little boy! Stop putting water into your boat! You are going to sink!"

At this point, Gina and I turned to see Mason holding a small water pail, the same pail he'd apparently been using to put one scoop of water at a time into the boat, which was now barely hovering above the surface. A few more scoops and we'd have surely gone down.

Frantically, we all started scooping up the water with our hands and pitching it back into the pond, until the boat eventually crept above water's surface, where it belonged.

But the memory is still vivid, that feeling that we might very well be going under, and not because of a flood, but because of a tiny pail…one scoop at a time.

Isn't that the way it is with sin? You add a little, then a little more, and then more and more, but in such small increments that you don't realize you are sinking, that the very vessel keeping you afloat is about to plunge beneath the surface and take you with it.

Thankfully, though we may not hear it in a booming voice screaming from speakers in the trees, we do still have the opportunity to hear the warning. We have God's Word on our hearts. We have the Holy Spirit to comfort us and guide us. We have fellow Christians to hold us accountable and to keep us from sinking. Or scoop us up when they see us start to go under.

This Week: Are you sinking slowly, one pail at a time, with your sin? More than likely, you won't have a voice screaming at you from the trees to tell you that you're drowning. But you have the Bible. You have prayer. You have the Holy Spirit. You have fellow Christians. You—are—not—alone. Grab hold of the One who cares and let Him save you from your sin.

MY PRAYER TO START THIS WEEK:

_____

_____

_____

_____

_____

THOSE TO REMEMBER IN PRAYER THIS WEEK:

_____

_____

_____

_____

_____

_____

_____

MONDAY, JULY 10

"NEVER BE LACKING IN ZEAL, *but keep your spiritual fervor, serving the Lord." Romans 12:11*

We have a squirrel in our chimney. Typically, squirrels don't bother me. In fact, I find them cute, fun to watch as they swish their tails and hide acorns and pecans in the trees in my back yard. But this squirrel…is in my chimney.

And he's loud. Scratching against the wall. Even sliding downward (we can hear him) as though he is going to pop out of the fireplace at any moment. This is particularly annoying in the middle of the night, since this chimney is in our bedroom.

During the winter, whenever we wanted a fire, we built one. And the squirrel would leave. For a while. Yet he always returned. He still always returns.

Clearly, I have no idea how to get rid of a squirrel in the chimney, but I have learned that a fire will make him leave for a little while. I imagine, if I could keep a fire burning year round, the squirrel would stay away.

Isn't that the same way it is with us? While our Christian fire is burning strong, the devil is held at bay. But then, our fire dies down…and he hurries back in to scratch against our walls, weaken our morals, try to make us forget that the fire lit by Christ is the only thing that will keep him away.

This Week: Stoke your Christian fire this week. Immerse yourself in God's Word. Surround yourself with God's people. Fill yourself with God's endless love.

MY PRAYER TO START THIS WEEK:

_____

_____

_____

_____

_____

_____

THOSE TO REMEMBER IN PRAYER THIS WEEK:

_____

_____

_____

_____

_____

_____

_____

MONDAY, JULY 17

"TRUTHFUL LIPS ENDURE FOREVER, BUT *a lying tongue lasts only a moment."* *Proverbs 12:19*

On July 15th last year, J.R. and I woke at 3:30am to drive to Vanderbilt Hospital in Nashville. We arrived in time to see Brittany, Matt's wife, and to learn the surgery would begin soon.

Matt, you may recall, is the young man who is like a son to us, and the one who I gave a kidney to five and a half years ago. On November 11, 2010, we had our transplant surgery, and I cried tears of joy when learning that the kidney had started working in the operating room.

But on this day, they were removing the kidney that had stopped working and, in fact, had starting hurting Matt with infection.

Matt wanted to talk to me before the surgery, and he wanted to see us after, and both times, he said the same thing. That he was sorry. As though this was his fault. It was, as the doctors said and in non-technical terms, "a fluke". The kidney should have lasted much longer, but an infection caused Matt's body to reject it, and now they were taking the organ out. Matt would go back on dialysis, and would pray to be put on the transplant list again.

At the hospital, everyone kept asking how I was doing. Some, like Matt, asked if I regretted donating the organ. I answered resolutely, "Never." I would do it again in a heartbeat. And if I could give Matt my other kidney now, I would. Like I said before, Matt is like a son to us. His wife like a daughter-in-law. His sons, our grandsons. I wouldn't trade anything for that.

But even after holding it together in front of everyone in the hospital, when I got in the car for the drive home…I couldn't stop crying. Not because I regretted giving the kidney, but because I truly wanted it to work for Matt for the remainder of his life. I liked knowing a part of me helped him live a normal life. And I was saddened to realize that was no longer the case. Plus, I had prayed. I'd been praying continually since learning the kidney was trying to fail. God had already given us a miracle, when we were a "perfect match" according to the physicians. Surely, He would give us another.

He didn't.

And I cried.

But then, as often the case, I assessed the situation and understood the monumental truth. God's ways are higher than mine. And He has a plan, even if I can't see it in my limited human scope. More than that, I understood another monumental truth: I trust Him. In the good, and in the bad, when I laugh, and when I cry, I trust Him.

This Week: Say this prayer: "Dear Lord, I trust You. I trust You in the good times, and I trust You in the bad. Cover me with peace, Lord. Let me feel Your love."

MY PRAYER TO START THIS WEEK:

_____

_____

_____

_____

_____

THOSE TO REMEMBER IN PRAYER THIS WEEK:

_____

_____

_____

_____

_____

_____

_____

MONDAY, JULY 24

" ALL SCRIPTURE IS GOD-BREATHED AND *is useful for teaching, rebuking, correcting and training in righteousness, so that the servant of God may be thoroughly equipped for every good work."* 2 Timothy 3:16-17

I have several writer friends who write continuities. The type of continuity I'm referring to is composed of a series of books that can each stand alone, but when combined, form a story that flows, with recurring characters and a central theme. To write a book in a continuity, authors rely on a "Book Bible," or a file composed of all of the characters that will be introduced in the series. Information about the town or city, landmarks, businesses, and so on are also provided to each author, so that when a reader works his or her way through the continuity, it appears as though it were written by one person.

But in continuities, it's easy to miss a minor detail, because you aren't the original author. Even if every character's eye color and hair color are correct, it's almost impossible to mimic the tone or nuances a previous author might have given a character. Plus, many times, the authors are all writing these books simultaneously, even if the release dates are months apart.

So mistakes happen.

Which makes me think about the Bible. The writers of the Bible got it all right though the story they told spanned years and writers and countries. God's Word is perfect, and we can rely on Him and the guidance He provided to its writers to guide us in our daily Christian walk.

My prayer life has strengthened over the years, and I also spend time enjoying devotionals and Bible studies written by others, but if there's an area where I know I could use more work, it would be spending time in God's Word, the Bible itself, rather than what someone says about it.

I'm going to make my best effort to change that.

This Week: Read one book of the Bible. And once you've finished, choose another. Devotions are awesome, but make certain you're going directly to the Source too. The Good News is always there, waiting for you to hear directly from your Lord.

MY PRAYER TO START THIS WEEK:

THOSE TO REMEMBER IN PRAYER THIS WEEK:

MONDAY, JULY 31

"IN THE SAME WAY, FAITH *by itself, if it is not accompanied by action, is dead." James 2:17*

My PawPaw Bowers kept a pill organizer in the center of the kitchen table. This was no ordinary pill organizer. It was huge, with three slots for each day's medicines (morning, noon and evening). The days were color-coded, and there were twenty-one slots (seven days, three times per day). Each Sunday, he would break out all of his pill bottles and start dropping the corresponding pills into the appropriate spots. He had red capsules, blue capsules, white, yellow…it looked like a rainbow of pills in the box each week.

Being young, I hated taking any kind of medicine and couldn't fathom why my grandfather didn't seem to mind this daily ritual. And it seemed he was always heading to John's Pharmacy, with our local pharmacist, to refill prescriptions. s he grew older, the number of pills increased, so that I didn't know how he swallowed them all without getting sick.

But those pills helped him. They controlled his cholesterol, his blood pressure and several other ailments and, without the medicine, he probably wouldn't have lived eighty-six years before passing on to his reward.

Back then, I didn't understand why he had to take all of those pills. But now that I've passed the half-century mark, I wake to take my cholesterol medicine (two capsules every morning) and end my day with cholesterol and thyroid medicine (two capsules for cholesterol, one pill for cholesterol and one pill for thyroid). Add to that the vitamins I take each day and a probiotic, and I'm tossing nine pills a day. Not as many as Paw Paw, but I'm still thirty years shy of his final years too. I have a feeling I might have a colorful, huge box too one day.

And I take those medicines for the same reason he did: they keep me healthy. Prolong life. Help me feel better each day.

What would happen if I had all of those medications…and merely read the labels? Would I be healthy? No. Would the medicine prolong my life? Definitely not. Would I feel better each day? I can answer that with a resounding no (I forgot my thyroid medicine on a vacation once and thought I'd be okay for a few days without it—wrong! I had to have my doctor call it in to a pharmacy nearby, because I felt like I was going to die right there. Clearly, I had no idea how important that tiny pill was to my feeling normal.)

In the same manner, as identified in the verse above, having faith without having action…is dead. We can't merely believe in God and do nothing about it, and expect our lives to be better, no more than we could read those medicine bottles and expect to be healthy.

This Week: If you're taking medicines on a daily basis, like me, make that a priority and don't "skip a day." Likewise, if you're a Christian, act on that faith…and don't "skip a day."

Note: *If you enjoy these devotions, please take a look at* **www.mondayswithjesus.com/** *to pre-order Mondays with Jesus 2018. You can purchase autographed, personalized copies for $9.99, the same price the book sells in stores, with free U.S. shipping* ☺ *I'd love to share my love of the Lord with you, your friends and relatives next year and hope that you'll see this book as an affordable option for your holiday gift-giving.*
Blessings always,

Renee

MY PRAYER TO START THIS WEEK:

_____

_____

_____

_____

_____

THOSE TO REMEMBER IN PRAYER THIS WEEK:

_____

_____

_____

_____

_____

_____

_____

MONDAY, AUGUST 7

"TAKE DELIGHT IN THE LORD, *and he will give you the desires of your heart. Commit your way to the Lord; trust in him and he will do this: He will make your righteous reward shine like the dawn, your vindication like the noonday sun." Psalm 37:4-6*

I have a Twitter account (**@ReneeAndrews**). If you follow me on Twitter, I'll go ahead and apologize, because I don't post that often. Most of the time, I will re-tweet what someone else has posted, often our son, Rene (**@ReneZeringue**), because he actually posts fairly regularly, and his words are most often spiritually uplifting and thought-provoking—things I want to share with my readers.

But recently, I did post a bit of text from a sermon that I found extremely inspiring. The gist of the message was how we need to trust God. If you're unfamiliar with Twitter, you may not know about the hashtags at the end of each tweet, but basically, in order to allow others to find your post based on subject matter, you can add a hashtag (#) at the end and follow it with text that highlights the subject or theme of the message.

So when I posted my message, I began to type the hashtag at the end and follow it with trustHim (**#trustHim**). Now, the computers are programmed to guess what you plan to type, right? So, as I began to type, my computer filled in the text with #trustnoone.

Trust No One.

I stared at the screen in disbelief. How sad, that in today's world, the most popular person to trust (at least in the program of my computer) is no one. Honestly, I can't remember hearing that at all when I grew up. If you heard the word "Trust," it was typically followed by, "God" or "in the Lord."

Quickly, I replaced the suggested text with what I intended: #TrustHim. And I will attempt to remind others—and myself—that my faith and my trust is in God.

This Week: If you're on social media of any type, post this verse: "Trust in the Lord with all your heart and lean not on your own understanding." Proverbs 3:5 #trustHim

MY PRAYER TO START THIS WEEK:

_____

_____

_____

_____

_____

THOSE TO REMEMBER IN PRAYER THIS WEEK:

_____

_____

_____

_____

_____

_____

_____

MONDAY, AUGUST 14

"*D*O NOT BE OVERCOME BY *evil, but overcome evil with good.*" *Romans 12:21*

My father's friend was driving down the interstate. He's known for his slow, careful driving, and he drives the interstate no differently, keeping his vehicle just below the speed limit. So, as he's driving along, a police officer pulled him over.

Their conversation went like this:

Officer: "Do you know why I pulled you over?"
Daddy's friend: "Because I was the only one you could catch?"

Sometimes in life, it feels as if we're the only one following the rules, driving the speed limit, following the law, doing what's right in God's eyes…while everyone else seems to be accelerating just as fast as they can, not only on the highways but also in life. Getting the bigger house, the fancier car, the better job, the beautiful clothes.

In fact, it often seems like those who don't follow the rules, those who cheat to get ahead, who lie and steal or do whatever is necessary to get what they want…are the ones who achieve success.

But the world's idea of success is a far cry from God's interpretation. Hebrews 11:25 describes the pleasures of sin as "fleeting." And Galatians 6:9 reminds us that "in due season we will reap, if we do not give up."

Success does come to God's people, even if it doesn't occur on this earth. In the end, we will have true success, an eternity with our Lord. And no fancy car, or job, or house…can compare to that!

This Week: List three people that you see as successful in the world's eyes. Now list three people that you deem successful in God's eyes. Note the differences in the way they live. What makes the first one happy? What makes the second one happy? Now…list three things that make you successful in God's eyes. And finally, what makes you happy?

MY PRAYER TO START THIS WEEK:

_____

_____

_____

_____

_____

_____

THOSE TO REMEMBER IN PRAYER THIS WEEK:

_____

_____

_____

_____

_____

_____

_____

_____

MONDAY, AUGUST 21

" FOR EVERYTHING IN THE WORLD—THE *lust of the flesh, the lust of the eyes, and the pride of life—comes not from the Father but from the world.*" 1 John 2:16

At the time I'm writing this devotion, my most recently released inspirational novel was *Family Wanted*. I put my heart into writing the book, primarily because it was the first in a series about children who had lost their parents, either due to being orphaned or abandoned, and I closely related to the story, since our oldest grandsons, Alanus and Jerry, were orphaned before our son and daughter-in-law adopted our precious grandboys.

So when the reviews started coming in for the book and then reader letters and emails followed, all thoroughly complimenting and praising the story, I have to admit that I felt a bit of pride. I'd written a book dear to my heart and it obviously resonated with readers, which is my secondary goal in writing Christian fiction (my first, of course, is to minister through my writing and glorify God).

But this time, with this book, I felt pride.

And so, when J.R. and I went to our post office box and I retrieved another reader letter, I said, "Look! Here's another reader touched by *Family Wanted*."

I tore open the letter and began reading it aloud.

And the woman tore me apart. She hated it, from the story theme to the writing to the ending. I'm actually surprised that she got to the ending, if she hated the story as much as she stated throughout her letter. The bottom line was that she couldn't forgive the heroine for the sins she committed in the beginning. Now, in my opinion, the forgiveness she achieved in the story held even more merit because of how far she'd moved herself from God. But this reader didn't see it that way, and she took over two pages of a handwritten letter to tell me just how very much she loathed it.

After I finished reading it, I looked to J.R. and said, "I was starting to feel prideful, and this lady just brought me back down to earth."

Pride is a dangerous thing and can catch you off-guard, especially when what you're feeling prideful about is actually something that glorifies God. I've heard preachers mention it before: that they struggle with wanting people know a message came from them rather than only caring about the fact that it is a message from God.

And though my goal with all of my writing is to glorify God, I need to take care that I remember: it is His glory, and His alone. I am merely an instrument to deliver His beautiful message.

This Week: When you feel your chest start to puff at a compliment, or start feeling a little too smugly about your abilities to do anything, remember that every good and perfect gift comes from the Lord, and the glory is His, and His alone.

MY PRAYER TO START THIS WEEK:

_____

_____

_____

_____

_____

THOSE TO REMEMBER IN PRAYER THIS WEEK:

_____

_____

_____

_____

_____

_____

_____

_____

MONDAY, AUGUST 28

"IURGE, THEN, FIRST OF ALL, *that petitions, prayers, intercession and thanksgiving be made for all people."* 1 Timothy 2:1

My husband is a mentor to many athletes. You might think this is because he is a former All-American gymnast, but while that might be why they seek him out for tumbling instruction, it isn't why they look up to him, to the point that they continue to stay in touch long after they're grown and have left our gym.

Since we purchased the first gym in 2008, his goal has been to share Christ and to be Christ-like to as many athletes as possible. To be a father figure to kids who may not have a father figure in the home. To show them about God's love by giving them a safe, Christian environment to exercise and improve their athletic abilities.

Over the years, several children have touched our hearts with their stories. Occasionally, one that has moved away will resurface, looking for guidance in the decisions faced in adulthood. Last summer, a former athlete needed employment. He was one of the most talented gymnasts J.R. ever coached, a boy who didn't have much growing up but did have God and trusted Him to provide everything He needed.

J.R. was glad to help him find a good job, and when we were visiting with him at his new city, we asked to pray over him and his new position. He told us to wait, so he could get his phone. He wanted to record our prayer, so that he could listen to it whenever he needed to hear it again.

I can tell you that, even as I type this now, I have tears. Nothing is more meaningful than understanding the power of prayer and seeing a young person understand it as well, to the point that he wants to have it at his fingertips at every opportunity. Yes, he can pray to God whenever he wants, but he also wanted to hear our prayers for him, and that meant the world to both of us.

You may never know who you're touching when you treat others as Christ would treat you. But then again, you may get the opportunity, as we did, to see how much that means, that you care, that you listen, and that you pray.

This Week: Become a mentor to someone younger than yourself. How? Listen. Care. Pray. It really is that simple. Be Christ-like, and they will see Christ reflected in you.

MY PRAYER TO START THIS WEEK:

_____

_____

_____

_____

_____

THOSE TO REMEMBER IN PRAYER THIS WEEK:

_____

_____

_____

_____

_____

_____

_____

MONDAY, SEPTEMBER 4

"SO THEY PULLED THEIR BOATS *up on shore, left everything and followed him." Luke 5:11*

I heard a story about a young woman filling out an application for college. She came upon the question, "Are you a leader?" Feeling the need to be honest, she answered...*No.*

Thinking she wouldn't hear from the university again, she forgot about the application. Then she received a letter that went like this:

"We have reviewed an abundance of applications and, to date, there will be around 1,467 new leaders attending school next year. We've decided to accept your application because we believe it is essential for every leader to have at least one follower."

Often in life, it appears as though being a follower isn't good enough. We should forge the way for others, stand out from the crowd, have everyone looking to us for answers. But ultimately, our most important goal shouldn't be to lead, but to follow—follow Christ. Just like those disciples did in the verse above, after Jesus asked them to lower their nets in the deep water, in spite of the fact that they'd fished all night and hadn't caught anything. Even so, they followed their Savior's command. And after they brought their boats to shore, they followed him—period.

We are to follow Christ, which also involves being a leader, when we lead others to Him. That's the kind of leader I want to be—a follower first, a leader second, and a daughter of the King always.

This Week: When asked if you are a follower or a leader, answer, "My goal is both. I strive to follow Christ, and to lead others to Him."

MY PRAYER TO START THIS WEEK:

_____

_____

_____

_____

_____

_____

THOSE TO REMEMBER IN PRAYER THIS WEEK:

_____

_____

_____

_____

_____

_____

_____

_____

MONDAY, SEPTEMBER 11

"TRULY I TELL YOU, WHATEVER *you did for one of the least of these brothers and sisters of mine, you did for me." Matthew 25:40*

J.R. came home from work wearing a beautiful new purple watch with gold accents. I knew I hadn't seen it before and asked him where he'd found it. He's from Baton Rouge and loves all things purple and gold, so I wasn't surprised at the hue of the watch; however, I'd never seen one like it.

He told me that over a year ago, he stopped to help a gentleman whose car had broken down. J.R. was driving his truck, which had an LSU tag on the front and one of the gym magnets advertising tour business on the back. The man showed up at our gym this week and gave the watch to him as a thank you. He said he'd never forgotten my husband's kindness and had been looking for a way to show his gratitude. He remembered that J.R. was an LSU fan, so when he saw the watch, he bought it and brought the gift to my sweet Cajun.

As J.R. told me the story (and I could see how much he loved the watch), I had to think about the fact that he followed Christ's instructions in Luke 6:31 that day, doing unto others as you'd have them do unto you. And I also wonder how many times Christians help someone and follow that example without even realizing the impact they are making in the other person's life. This man searched an entire year for the perfect way to say thanks.

This Week: Look for the opportunities Christ gives you to help others. The purple watch is awesome, but the opportunity to show someone that Christ is living in you is priceless.

MY PRAYER TO START THIS WEEK:

_____

_____

_____

_____

_____

_____

THOSE TO REMEMBER IN PRAYER THIS WEEK:

_____

_____

_____

_____

_____

_____

_____

MONDAY, SEPTEMBER 18

"THE KING WILL REPLY, 'TRULY *I tell you, whatever you did for one of the least of these brothers and sisters of mine, you did for me."*
Matthew 25:40

On Valentine's Day of 2014, the University of Alabama in Birmingham (UAB) football team had an off-season workout at Legion Field in Birmingham. One of the players, Tim Alexander, had been a part of the program for several years, but he wasn't taking part as the team climbed the stairs to the stadium. He couldn't. Tim had been paralyzed in a car crash. But he was at every practice and every game wearing number 87.

On this day, however, Tim didn't remain at the bottom of the stadium while his teammates made the climb to the top, because the Strength and Conditioning coach, a man by the name of Zac Woodfin, started carrying Tim up the stairs. And after the coach began carrying the paralyzed player, the other teammates joined in to help Coach Woodfin take their teammate to the top.

What a beautiful example of the way we should love, the way we should serve. And I loved the fact that, when the teammates saw their coach acting like Christ, they joined in the journey.

Isn't that the way we should all be? Looking for the one left out, the one who needs to be carried at times, and then joining in to help along the journey? That's what Christ would do...and that's what we should do.

This Week: When you see someone left out of the group, do what you can to bring them in. If they're standing at the bottom, in any situation, do what you can to carry them to the top. You never know; you may find an entire team standing nearby and ready to help you on the journey.

MY PRAYER TO START THIS WEEK:

THOSE TO REMEMBER IN PRAYER THIS WEEK:

MONDAY, SEPTEMBER 25

"*So we must listen very carefully to the truth we have heard, or we may drift away from it.*" *Hebrews 2:1*

When Rene and Kaleb were growing up, one of their favorite vacation places was a campground on Myrtle Beach. We would go there nearly every summer, usually around the Fourth of July. The campground hosted church youth groups throughout the summer, and each weekday, the group would have a Vacation Bible School on the beach. The boys loved it.

One of the other things they enjoyed about Myrtle Beach was the waves, so much higher than those on the gulf. They liked taking their boogie boards out and riding those waves. When they were little, we didn't let them go out into the water without us beside them, but as they got older, we eventually let them play on their own, while we kept a close eye from the shore.

However, in spite of our directive for them to stay in the water in front of where we sat, they would drift down the beach with the current. J.R. and I would see them moving away and do our mad dash down the beach to rein them back in and have them move to their original location. Then, without fail, after a bit of playing, they wouldn't pay attention to the shore and would find themselves farther down the beach...while we would yell to get their attention and, once again, herd them back to the proper position.

It is easy to drift away if we aren't paying attention. This is especially true when we are trying to wade into the waters of the world and take our eyes off of the shore, take our attention off of the One who cares and let ourselves get pulled away.

The thing about drifting is that you don't realize it's happening. It's a slow process, but one that inevitably causes you to be separated from your original location completely.

This Week: If you're drifting away, even if only slightly, turn back toward the One who cares. Listen to those that love you and are calling you home. They aren't trying to hurt you; they are trying to save you. And if you know someone drifting away, don't merely let them go. Bring them back in—show them they have you, and remind them they have a Savior!

MY PRAYER TO START THIS WEEK:

_____

_____

_____

_____

_____

_____

THOSE TO REMEMBER IN PRAYER THIS WEEK:

_____

_____

_____

_____

_____

_____

_____

_____

MONDAY, OCTOBER 2

"**B**ARNABAS WANTED TO TAKE JOHN, *also called Mark, with them, but Paul did not think it wise to take him, because he had deserted them in Pamphylia and had not continued with them in the work. They had such a sharp disagreement that they parted company. Barnabas took Mark and sailed for Cyprus, but Paul chose Silas and left, commended by the believers to the grace of the Lord. He went through Syria and Cilicia, strengthening the churches."* Acts 15:37-41

My father used this story often when I was growing up and would have disagreements with friends. I was a typical teenage girl, or at least I think it was typical, in that I was very intimidated by other teen girls. If a group started whispering when I neared, I thought they were talking about me. If someone (or several) stopped speaking to me altogether, I would wonder what I'd done to upset them.

Is that typical for a teen girl? I sure hope so, or else I put my parents through a lot of unnecessary misery.

But in any case, I remember Daddy bringing up the story of Paul and Barnabas and how they agreed to disagree, with regard to bringing John Mark on their journey.

Nowadays, I don't find myself in the same type of situations as high school, where I'm so self-conscious about the comments of others. But I do still deal with those who choose not to be a friend. And by "friend," I don't mean it in the physical sense, like I would've meant when I was in school. I mean it in the digital sense, as in online, or Facebook. People will "unfriend" or "unfollow" an individual to show that they no longer like the person or something that person stands for. I've actually had this happen to me a few times—and in each instance, I didn't notice the person was no longer a "friend" until they told me. And then sent me a new friend request.

The situations were much different than high school. One individual was upset with a friend of mine, and therefore de-friended all of her friends. The other one didn't like seeing information about my family, because their own family was quite broken, and it made that person sad to see another family that seemed to have it all together (note the "seemed to" in that sentence—no family is perfect, because no person is perfect; there is only One that was.)

But thankfully, with the ones who unfriended me for a time, we were each still pursuing our Heavenly Father, in spite of the fact that we were no longer "friends". And what I love about the story of Paul and Barnabas is that, even though they chose to go different routes, they both still continued pursuing their Heavenly Father. And, in their case, because they separated, we can assume that even more people learned about Christ. How amazing is that?

This Week: If you have someone you simply can't agree with, don't let that hinder each of you from continuing your Christian walk. In fact, use that separation to reach even more people for Christ the way Paul and Barnabas did back then.

MY PRAYER TO START THIS WEEK:

_____

_____

_____

_____

_____

THOSE TO REMEMBER IN PRAYER THIS WEEK:

_____

_____

_____

_____

_____

_____

_____

MONDAY, OCTOBER 9

"THEREFORE, IF ANYONE IS IN *Christ, the new creation has come: The old has gone, the new is here."* *2 Corinthians 5:17*

Kaleb and Kaiyla, our youngest son and daughter-in-law, recently bought their first house. It was built in the 1940s and had been in the same family for over forty years. The elderly woman that had lived there raised her family in the house, but hadn't done much to the home physically since she and her husband began living there in 1970. So the place needed plenty of work. It had cracks in the ceilings and walls, as well as the effects of frying. We live in the South, where frying is a regular part of cooking, and according to the lady's children, she fried *something* for *every* meal. As a result, the kitchen cabinets and walls had a coating of grease. The ceiling fan, in fact, had collected so much grease over the years that it had adhered to the ceiling in a gummy muck.

Needless to say, they got a great deal on the house due to the condition. But what hooked them wasn't necessarily the potential of fixing up the old place, but the way that the children, now in their sixties, spoke of growing up there. They talked about visiting on the screened-in porch, sharing family meals, the Christmases they shared in the home (there was a Christmas tree in the attic that was still fully decorated), and Kaleb and Kaiyla could see the potential for raising their own family in the home.

As I write this, we're all still working on the renovations; it's definitely a family affair. They bought the home in June, and it's October, so we're drawing near the end and preparing for them to move in. And the house is, quite honestly, amazing. You see, as they started tearing out the old walls, they found a brick chimney from an old pot-belly stove that had been completely hidden. Additionally, after they pulled up the carpet, and then linoleum, and then parquet...they found the original, quite beautiful, hardwood floors.

And in their restoration process, the old house has become "new" again, something beautiful to be appreciated.

Isn't that the way it is with Christ? When He touches something old and neglected, like us—and the sins of our past—He can make us new. Something beautiful. Something to be appreciated. Because, like Kaleb and Kaiyla care about their house, He cares about us and wants to give us another chance, a fresh start. All we have to do…is let Him have his way.

This Week: When you drive, think about how difficult it would be to go forward if you spent the entire time looking in the rearview mirror. Then stop looking in the rearview mirror of your past. Look to your future, to the "new" that only Christ can give you, and move forward.

MY PRAYER TO START THIS WEEK:

_____

_____

_____

_____

_____

_____

THOSE TO REMEMBER IN PRAYER THIS WEEK:

_____

_____

_____

_____

_____

_____

_____

_____

MONDAY, OCTOBER 16

" IF YOU REALLY KEEP THE *royal law found in Scripture, "Love your neighbor as yourself," you are doing right." James 2:8*

Does your home have a porch? My past three homes haven't had a porch; each had a deck, but no porch. That seems to be the trend nowadays. Homes have a deck across the back, a place to gather with family and enjoy grilling or visiting, but it's confined to the back of the house, most often with some type of privacy fence protecting the occupants from the outside world.

This is so different than the style of home I enjoyed growing up. My grandmother's house had an amazing porch. I remember it had a concrete floor, painted blue. The ceiling was also blue. Recently, I learned that painting a porch ceiling blue helps keep the spiders and bugs away, because they think it is the sky. I have no idea if that's why Granny's ceiling and floor were blue, but they were.

In any case, we spend many days and nights on that porch. When we went to visit, we didn't gather on a deck in the back or in front of a television indoors, we would head to the porch. Granny had a porch swing, some rockers and chairs. There were big silver washtubs that we would use for shucking corn, shelling purple hull peas and snapping green beans. We also had plastic trays that were used for eating watermelon. And the old wooden ice cream maker (with a crank!) sat nearby. Neighbors were always out walking or riding bicycles through the farm-focused neighborhood, and they would wave or stop and chat.

But in modern times, people keep to themselves and often do not even know the names of their neighbors next door. How can we "love our neighbor" if we don't know who they are? How can we care for others as Christ cares for us? How can we truly be Christ-like if we seclude ourselves from the world?

We recently moved back to that neighborhood of my youth. The house has a porch, not nearly as big as my Granny's porch, but big enough for a couple of chairs. I've been sitting in a chair on this front porch to write, because it gives me peace, and the stories flow. But more than that, I have met at least a dozen neighbors who were walking past, or driving, or riding a bicycle. They have their children or grandchildren with them, and they all say hello. They want to know about my family. They care. It's easy to communicate and get to know others when we make ourselves approachable, isn't it? And it's easy to treat others like Christ would treat them too.

This Week: If you have a front porch, take some time to sit there and see if you can't meet some of those neighbors nearby. If you don't have one, find another way to meet your neighbors. Invite them over to grill out, or take them a casserole. If you need a delicious (and easy) recipe, send me an email, and I'll share a poppy seed chicken casserole recipe that is a cinch to make and usually a crowd pleaser.☺ Be a neighbor today! Be like Christ today!

MY PRAYER TO START THIS WEEK:

_____

_____

_____

_____

_____

THOSE TO REMEMBER IN PRAYER THIS WEEK:

_____

_____

_____

_____

_____

_____

_____

MONDAY, OCTOBER 23

"AND HE DIED FOR ALL, *that those who live should no longer live for themselves but for him who died for them and was raised again."* 2 Corinthians 5:15

Living in my hometown again, I run into people and families I've known for years. It's always enjoyable to see my friends from high school in their different aspects of life. Most of us are moving into the grandparent age now, and I've truly enjoyed sharing those photos of my grandbabies and seeing my friends' photos of theirs at all of our reunions.

But occasionally, I will see or hear of a friend whose life didn't follow a normal course. I've had a couple of classmates from high school who turned to drugs or alcohol during difficult times. One had a drug-related death. Three chose lives of crime and have either previously served jail time or are currently serving prison sentences (they have been in and out of jail over the thirty-plus years since we graduated high school).

Have you ever thought about the fact that *live* spelled backwards is *evil?* When we don't live the way we should, when we don't have Christ as a part of our life and try to live as He would have us to, then we're living backwards, heading the wrong direction. Our attempt to *live* becomes *evil.*

It is sad to learn that someone you know has been living backwards, but hopeful to think that they don't have to continue. At least one of my classmates who ended up in prison after high school has completely turned his life around. I will pray for the others to do the same and will do whatever I can to help that to happen.

This Week: Undoubtedly, you know someone who is living their life backwards. Pray for them. Send a card of encouragement. Help them find Christ…through you.

MY PRAYER TO START THIS WEEK:

_____

_____

_____

_____

_____

THOSE TO REMEMBER IN PRAYER THIS WEEK:

_____

_____

_____

_____

_____

_____

MONDAY, OCTOBER 30

"DO NOT LET ANY UNWHOLESOME *talk come out of your mouths, but only what is helpful for building others up according to their needs, that it may benefit those who listen." Ephesians 4:29*

In the summer of 1979, Randy VanWarmer released a hit song with what I believed was one of the most beautiful melodies I'd ever heard. I was only thirteen at the time, but I told my mother that the song was so pretty that I wanted it played at my wedding one day.

I still remember her trying not to laugh and then asking me if I'd listened to the words. Obviously, I hadn't:

"You left me…just when I needed you most."

If you're anywhere near my age, you're probably hearing the melody now. It was beautiful. But definitely not the words meant to accompany the pledging of wedding vows. And, like my mom, I'm trying not to laugh about how I thought it was the perfect wedding song at the time.

But words can definitely change the meaning of things, right? In fact, some words can scar a relationship for life. Yes, you can forgive, and you can pray to forget, but the memory of hurtful words can haunt that relationship forever. I've been guilty of this, saying something and then instantly wishing I could push those words back in my mouth. Or that the person listening might be able to forget, which rarely happens.

Therefore, I pray for God to help guide my tongue, to control it, and to control the thoughts that cause me to say things that shouldn't have ever been said.

This Week: My husband is great at waiting a moment before he answers or speaks. I can actually see him thinking about what he is going to say. I've never been that way and tend to blurt whatever is on my mind. But I'm going to try to do a bit of thinking before the words leave my mouth. I'll encourage you to as well (though, most likely, you're already better than me ;)

MY PRAYER TO START THIS WEEK:

_____

_____

_____

_____

_____

THOSE TO REMEMBER IN PRAYER THIS WEEK:

_____

_____

_____

_____

_____

_____

_____

_____

MONDAY, NOVEMBER 6

"For if you forgive other *people when they sin against you, your heavenly Father will also forgive you. But if you do not forgive others their sins, your Father will not forgive your sins." Matthew 6:14-15*

My preacher, Wayne Dunaway, recently made a statement that truly resonated with me:

"Don't bury the hatchet and leave the handle sticking up."

It may be easy to say, "I forgive you," or it may be tough. Truthfully, it is much easier for me to say those words to someone I love. Most of the time, the words aren't even needed, because I forgive instantly when it's someone I care about. I love them enough to understand that they aren't perfect, as I hope that they love me enough to do the same, because I am so very far from perfect.

But when it isn't someone I care about, a loved one or family member, it's a little more difficult to say the words and actually follow through, truly forgive, as in never bringing up the offense again. Or, if not bringing it up, thinking about it every time you hear that person's name.

We say we bury the hatchet, but if we leave the handle sticking up so we can grab onto it again at any given opportunity, then we haven't truly buried it. Buried means covered completely. Unseen. Forgotten.

Granted, we may not find it possible to forget an offense completely, but we can find it in our hearts to do our best. Don't hold onto the wrong, thinking about it so that it festers and irritates until…we grab that handle and swing the hatchet once more.

If we forgive others, as indicated in the verse above, our Heavenly Father will forgive us. And if we don't, neither will he.

This Week: If you're having trouble truly forgiving, pray. Ask for God's help, and let it go. Bury that hatchet—completely.

MY PRAYER TO START THIS WEEK:

_____

_____

_____

_____

_____

THOSE TO REMEMBER IN PRAYER THIS WEEK:

_____

_____

_____

_____

_____

_____

_____

MONDAY, NOVEMBER 13

"BUT WHEN THE SET TIME *had fully come, God sent his Son, born of a woman, born under the law, to redeem those under the law, that we might receive adoption to sonship. Because you are his sons, God sent the Spirit of his Son into our hearts, the Spirit who calls out, "Abba, Father." So you are no longer a slave, but God's child; and since you are his child, God has made you also an heir."* Galatians 4:4-7

I've often wondered how God sees me. Since He is omniscient, omnipresent and omnipotent, there isn't anything He doesn't see or know. And that would seem a good thing, until I wouldn't want Him seeing everything I think, everything I do. I know I'm not perfect, but at times, I feel so far removed from it that I'm not worthy of Him even being interested in my world.

Do you ever feel that you closely relate to Paul, as he spoke to the Romans in Romans 7:15?

"I do not understand what I do. For what I want to do I do not do, but what I hate I do."

I know I feel that way at times, and it hits me hard, the guilt of not living up to what I want to be for my Lord. And I wonder…what does He see at that moment, when He looks at me?

The question brings to mind my birthdays each year growing up, when my Nanny Lankford (my maternal grandmother) would bring my favorite dessert. It was a chocolate cake that she made from scratch, the most amazing chocolate cake I've ever eaten to this day (and unfortunately, I never got the recipe). She made the fudge icing that coated the cake, as well as the white divinity filling between each layer. I can almost taste that cake now, just thinking about it. In my mind, that cake was… perfect.

But one year, on my birthday, Nanny was bringing the cake over and turned more sharply than she intended on the curve to our driveway. As a result, the cake carrier slid off the seat, the chocolate cake slammed into the side and icing smeared against the container.

Nanny came in the house with tears tumbling down her cheeks. In her mind, she'd ruined my birthday present. But I was chomping at the bit to open that cake carrier. Did the cake look like it usually did? No, but I didn't care. I knew my Nanny had spent her entire day working on each stage of that cake, and I knew it would taste just as delicious as it always did (and it did, by the way). I wasted no time hugging her and then asking if we could all have a piece (or two – hey, I was the birthday girl). And even though I could see that the cake wasn't perfect, it still looked perfect in my eyes. Because Nanny made it, and because I knew that, on the inside, it was still the same.

I like knowing that, when God looks at me, and I feel as though I've slid off the path and been slammed into the side of something, much like that chocolate cake, He sees what's inside. He knows everything, so He knows my heart. He knows I'm doing my best and that I pray to Him to help me do my best always. And He knows that, if I had my way, every day I'd be as good…as my Nanny's chocolate cake.

This Week: Have a piece of chocolate cake. Think about the fact that, whether all of the layers are lined up perfectly or have tumbled into a big lumpy mess, it still tastes the same—delicious!.

MY PRAYER TO START THIS WEEK:

_____

_____

_____

_____

_____

_____

THOSE TO REMEMBER IN PRAYER THIS WEEK:

_____

_____

_____

_____

_____

_____

_____

_____

MONDAY, NOVEMBER 20

"DECLARE HIS GLORY AMONG THE *nations, his marvelous deeds among all peoples." Psalm 96:3*

Catherine, one of the preschoolers in our gym, loves her gymnastics class. She can't wait each week to see her friends and visit with her coaches. But this week, she was too excited to concentrate on the task at hand.

"I can't tumble yet," she explained to my husband.

"Why can't you tumble yet, Catherine?" J.R. asked.

"Because I'm too excited! I have to tell you about my Disney trip first!"

And so J.R. listened to all of the details about her trip, and *then* they began her tumbling lesson.

I can remember times in my life when I couldn't wait to share my news: when I got my driver's license, when I received my scholarship to college, when I got my first job, when J.R. proposed, when we were married and when we had children. That list continues to grow, with the most recent bursts of good news occurring when we welcome a new grandchild into the family.

There's nothing quite like that feeling of excitement when you have something so good to tell that you simply can't wait to share the news.

But the best news of all is at our fingertips every day and should be on the tip of our tongue every day as well. The Good News of Christ. His triumph over death. His triumph over sin. Our hope because of Him!

Praise God for that amazingly Good News, and let me remember that there is no better news to share than our Lord!

This Week: Share the Good News of your Lord and Savior with the same kind of can't-wait excitement that Catherine shared the news of her trip! No... with even more excitement! Because what better news is there than Christ!

MY PRAYER TO START THIS WEEK:

_____

_____

_____

_____

_____

_____

THOSE TO REMEMBER IN PRAYER THIS WEEK:

_____

_____

_____

_____

_____

_____

_____

MONDAY, NOVEMBER 27

"WHAT YOU HAVE SEEN WITH *your eyes do not bring hastily to court, for what will you do in the end if your neighbor puts you to shame?" Proverbs 25:8*

I don't know about where you live, but for us in the South, November and December are months for pie, specifically pecan pie. My Granny Bowers and Nanny Lankford both made the most amazing pecan pies. Thankfully, my mother has continued the tradition (I should probably learn how to make one of those pies). Right now, just typing about it and knowing that mom will most likely be making one in the next few weeks has my mouth watering.

But I remember one Thanksgiving when my Granny Bowers wanted the grandkids to try something different. We all loved the pecan pie, but we would rarely go for a slice of the pumpkin or sweet potato ones that also donned her long wooden buffet during the holidays.

So on this particular Thanksgiving, we all went for the pecan pie as usual, but it tasted different. And we soon found out why. Determined to get us to try something new, Granny had placed pecans…across the top of her pumpkin pie.

I don't think any of us decided we liked pumpkin pie merely because of the pecans on top, but we never looked at Granny's dessert spread the same way again. Who knew what was hiding beneath those pecans?

In the same manner, I've seen things in life that appear to be one thing and then, once I delved beneath the surface, were something different entirely. This doesn't merely apply to things, but to people. Someone can have a façade that seems genuine—even Christian—while hiding quite the opposite beneath the surface. Likewise, others may not seem spiritual at all, yet be downright angelic, once you give them a chance.

It's difficult to see someone and not jump to some sort of conclusion. I think of the old saying, "You never get a second chance to make a first impression." But the Bible warns us repeatedly about the dangers of jumping to conclusions. In Joshua 22:9-34, the Israelites almost went to war because of it. And I've almost missed the chance at getting to know some amazing people because I caught myself judging a book by its cover.

I pray that God helps me keep an open mind and an open heart when I'm meeting His children. That's what Christ did, when he met those whom others would consider unsavory. Tax collectors. The Samaritan woman. The woman caught in adultery. He met some unique and amazing people…because He knew what was hidden beneath the surface.

Lord, help me to remember You and to delve deeper as I get to know Your children.

This Week: Say, "Hello," to a dozen strangers (or more). If speaking goes way too far outside of your comfort zone, offer a smile.

MY PRAYER TO START THIS WEEK:

_____

_____

_____

_____

_____

THOSE TO REMEMBER IN PRAYER THIS WEEK:

_____

_____

_____

_____

_____

_____

_____

MONDAY, DECEMBER 4

"WHOEVER CLAIMS TO LIVE IN *him must live as Jesus did.*" 1 *John 2:6*

Yesterday, I received a phone call that brought me to tears. The woman has a little boy who takes gymnastics classes at our gym. He's been at the gym a few months and, because he comes later in the evening, I have yet to meet the boy. But I did know his story from when she shared it with me on the day she signed him up for classes.

He came from an abusive family, to the point that he suffered post-traumatic stress disorder (PTSD) from the past abuse. He had been a foster child in her home for a while, but recently, her family had been blessed to legally adopt the boy. However, he still had a difficult time trusting people, often seemed withdrawn and had problems with self-esteem due to what he'd been through before.

But as she called to make sure our gym was open yesterday afternoon (our local schools were closed for the day, but the gym was still open), she told me how happy she was to learn we were still having classes. "He looks forward to that class each week. It has really changed him. He feels better about himself and has truly started coming out of his shell, and I have to tell you that your son, Kaleb, has made a huge impact on his life. He's such a positive example and role model for him, and my son can't wait to see him each week. I can't tell you how much that means to me."

Kaleb, like my husband, competed in gymnastics, but more than enjoying the sport, he loves the opportunity to minister to children through his coaching at the gym. Kaleb is twenty-five but well beyond his years when it comes to relating to these children. This is not the first parent who has called to let me know how he is impacting their child, and let me tell you, as a mom, it doesn't get much better than to see Christ reflected in your son. Praise God!

This Week: Until I told Kaleb last night, he had no idea what that little boy had been through or how much of a difference he'd made in his world. And you may not know the lives you will touch as you treat others as Christ would treat you. Be the light in their world today.

MY PRAYER TO START THIS WEEK:

_____

_____

_____

_____

_____

THOSE TO REMEMBER IN PRAYER THIS WEEK:

_____

_____

_____

_____

_____

_____

_____

MONDAY, DECEMBER 11

" IN EVERYTHING I DID, I *showed you that by this kind of hard work we must help the weak, remembering the words the Lord Jesus himself said: It is more blessed to give than to receive." Matthew 6:2-4*

This is the season where we are reminded continually of our Lord. His name is prevalent throughout, with every storefront typically displaying something to remind us of Christmas. Lighted trees and evergreen wreaths abound, as do thought-provoking manger scenes and an assortment of crosses.

Gift-giving, of course, is a prominent tradition at this time of year.

I keep an ongoing list on my phone of items my children and grandchildren might enjoy—nothing overly expensive, but little things they mention in passing. And it does make me feel good when they open a small gift and then wonder how I knew (you have to listen closely in this family—it's tough for me to get them to tell me anything that they want).

But I love that feeling of giving, and I know the emotion associated with the action is undoubtedly God-given, hence the verse above.

Dr. Chester Hicks, a friend and a member of our life group (small group Bible study) gave a beautiful example of the importance of giving at one of our recent Bible studies. He and his wife, Martha, have visited the Bible lands on several occasions. I've always wanted to visit the places where Jesus walked, so I enjoy hearing about their trips. At our Bible study, Dr. Hicks spoke about the contrasts of the two bodies of water where Jesus lived, the Sea of Galilee and the Dead Sea.

The Sea of Galilee is stunning, thirteen miles long and eight miles wide plentiful with fish and lush foliage. It is undeniably beautiful, with its water flowing to feed into the Jordan River, which then feeds into the Dead Sea. The Dead Sea, on the other hand, is symbolic with its name. You will not see any fish or anything else swimming in the water. The salt content is so extensive that it is ten times saltier than any other ocean in the world. In fact, anything that might accidentally swim into the Dead Sea from the freshwater streams that feed into it is killed instantly. The water is stagnant and allows nothing to survive.

The two bodies of water are merely separated by the Jordan River. It would seem they would be similar in foliage and fish species. But the Sea of Galilee is a giving body of water, feeding into the Jordan River and thus also feeding into the Dead Sea. In contrast, the Dead Sea merely receives water from other streams. It doesn't give, and therefore doesn't move. And everything in it...dies.

What an excellent example of the Biblical truth: it is indeed more blessed to give than to receive.

This Week: Give something thoughtful this week. It doesn't have to be expensive. A card. A handwritten note. A smile. Experience the joy of how blessed it feels to give.

MY PRAYER TO START THIS WEEK:

_____

_____

_____

_____

_____

THOSE TO REMEMBER IN PRAYER THIS WEEK:

_____

_____

_____

_____

_____

_____

_____

MONDAY, DECEMBER 18

"THEN THE WORD OF THE *Lord came to Jonah a second time.*"
Jonah 3:1

Withdraw passing. I was quite familiar with that term during college, because I began my four years with the goal of graduating with a perfect 4.0. Therefore, if I neared the middle of a semester and didn't have an "A" in the class (and wasn't certain I could get there by the semester's end), I would head to the registrar's office and ask for a *Withdraw Passing Form*. I would receive no credit for the course, but I also wouldn't have anything less than an "A" on my record (can you say…perfectionist?).

The next semester, I would retake the class and (hopefully) get the grade I wanted. Now, it's important to note that I did *not* graduate with a 4.0. The thing was, I met my Cajun and decided I'd rather take a lower grade, graduate and get married than stay in school in pursuit of a 4.0.

But I definitely used my second chances…a few times. Recently, when reading the book of Jonah, I noticed—really noticed—the verse above. The word of the Lord came to Jonah *a second time*. Granted, I was happy that my university gave me the opportunity to give those classes another go, but I am absolutely elated that my Lord and Savior does the same thing! God had spoken to Jonah, told him exactly what to do with regard to the Ninevites, and when he didn't…God spoke to him a second time. Gave him another chance. True, he spent time in a big fish during the interim, but still…God gave him a second chance.

And, praise God, He gives us second chances too. Because none of us get it right the first time. I'd begin listing my mistakes and the times I've needed second chances, but that list would formulate a book of its own (probably a multi-volume series).

However, I can delight in the fact that God knows me, He knows my heart, and He gives me second chances.

This Week: Think of your most recent biggest mistake (if you're like me, there isn't merely one to choose from). Thank God that He understands and gives a second chance.

MY PRAYER TO START THIS WEEK:

THOSE TO REMEMBER IN PRAYER THIS WEEK:

MONDAY, DECEMBER 25

"WHILE THEY WERE THERE, THE *time came for the baby to be born, and she gave birth to her firstborn, a son. She wrapped him in cloths and placed him in a manger, because there was no guest room available for them."* Luke 2:6-7

I'm writing this devotion while holding our newest grandson, Konrad Asher Zeringue. At the time I'm writing this, he's just over four months old, still fairly new to the world, his eyes starting to focus on us and his mouth just starting to smile when he recognizes my face. Such a precious, sweet smile.

But on the morning of his birth, things didn't go as smoothly as we'd hoped. While Kaiyla was in labor, J.R. and I went to the room to visit with her and Kaleb as we awaited the precious baby's birth…and Kaiyla looked to Kaleb and told him something wasn't right. Then one of the machines began to beep, and then two nurses came in and shuffled us out of the room, with other nurses heading that direction.

Konrad's heart had stopped, and the nurses didn't know why. They started twisting and turning Kaiyla because they thought something might be happening with the umbilical cord, and with a couple of fierce turns, his heart began beating again.

The next hours were filled with prayer. The families sat in the waiting room attempting to stay calm but praying and begging God to protect our littlest angel. And then, when the doctor arrived and Kaiyla started delivering the baby…his heart stopped again. And the doctor had to rush to bring Konrad into the world.

The whirlwind of events that morning only lasted a few hours, but it seemed to take forever, due to the intensity of our prayer. We wanted to see that sweet baby, to hold him and praise God for him…and we cried tears of joy when we did.

Can you imagine the apprehension Joseph and Mary felt at seeing their child—the Son of God? The tears of joy as they held Him, praised God for Him and cried tears of joy for Him?

Praise God today for our precious Savior's birth. Praise God today for the season where everyone has our Lord at the front of their thoughts. Praise God today for every good and perfect gift, because every gift, every life—every breath—comes from Him!

Thank You, Jesus!

This Week: Celebrate the beauty of the birth of our Lord! Celebrate His life, His death and His glorious resurrection, not just in this season but in every season!

MY PRAYER TO START THIS WEEK:

_____

_____

_____

_____

_____

THOSE TO REMEMBER IN PRAYER THIS WEEK:

_____

_____

_____

_____

_____

_____

_____

_____

DEDICATIONS

For my parents, James and Jolaine Bowers.
God blessed me with you!

OTHER BOOKS AVAILABLE

AUTHOR BIO

National Readers' Choice Award winner and RT Reviewers' Choice Award winner Renee Andrews spends a lot of time in the gym. No, she isn't working out. Her husband, a former All-American gymnast, owns a cheerleading and tumbling gym. She is thankful the talented kids at the gym don't have a problem when she brings her laptop and writes while they sweat. When she isn't writing, she's typically traveling with her husband, bragging about their sons and daughters-in-law or spoiling their grandchildren.

Renee is a kidney donor and actively supports organ donation. In 2013, Renee, her husband J.R. and their oldest son Rene competed as team Hello Kidney on the American Bible Challenge to raise money for living donors and to raise awareness for the need for living donors. If you are considering becoming a living donor, ask her about how you can also save a life by sharing your spare. Or check out the "living donor" section of her website.

She welcomes prayer requests and loves to hear from readers. Write her at Renee@ReneeAndrews.com or visit her at her website.

Renee Andrews on Facebook:
www.facebook.com/AuthorReneeAndrews
Renee Andrews on Twitter:
www.twitter.com/ReneeAndrews
To purchase autographed copies of Renee's devotionals, visit
www.MondayswithJesus.com

www.ingramcontent.com/pod-product-compliance
Lightning Source LLC
Chambersburg PA
CBHW031533040426
42445CB00010B/523